Jan 2016

THE WHOLE ENCHILADA

THE WHOLE ENCHILADA

FRESH AND NUTRITIOUS SOUTHWESTERN CUISINE

....

ANGELINA LARUE

....

PHOTOGRAPHY BY **DEBORAH WHITLAW LLEWELLYN**

PELICAN PUBLISHING COMPANY

Gretna 2015

The word "Pelican" and the depiction of a pelican are
trademarks of Pelican Publishing Company, Inc., and are
registered in the U.S. Patent and Trademark Office.

Design and production by Janice Shay / Pinafore
Photography by Deborah Whitlaw Llewellyn
Additional photography: Texas Deptartment of
Transportation; Kevin Stillman/TxDOT, p. 45
Geoff Appold/TxDOT, p.169

ISBN: 9781455620692
E-book ISBN: 9781455620708

Printed in China
Published by Pelican Publishing Company, Inc.
1000 Burmaster Street, Gretna, Louisiana 70053

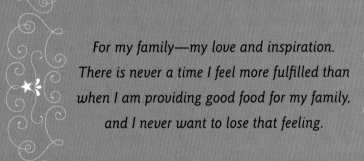

For my family—my love and inspiration.
There is never a time I feel more fulfilled than
when I am providing good food for my family,
and I never want to lose that feeling.

TABLE OF CONTENTS

INTRODUCTION

SOUTHWESTERN CUISINE has made its way into many regions of the country and is gaining a huge following nationwide. Whether you've headed to 6th Street in Austin for a late-night taco, visited the festive town square in Sante Fe to dine on blue-corn enchiladas, or found your way to a local eatery that serves up some great salsa and queso, the recipes in this book will allow you to enjoy tasty Tex-Mex and Southwestern food in your own *cocina*.

As a food columnist, recipe developer, and blogger, I share my love for this regional cuisine on a broad scale. While being raised in West Texas, I was fortunate to partake in the beautiful, fresh produce grown by my family of gardeners and farmers. I was blessed to be inspired by hardworking women who turned out scrumptious Southern food, meal after meal. At the same time, my cooking style has been heavily influenced by the Tex-Mex and Mexican flavors of the Southwest. The mesquite-smoked goodness billowing from PaPaw's Texas smoker, and a sprinkling of Native American Indian flavors from the region also helped form my style of cooking, and these recipes.

Mexican food, and especially Tex-Mex, can often get a bad rap for being calorie-packed, cheese-heavy meals. My usual rule is: The fresher and lighter the ingredients, the healthier the food will be. Make no mistake, there's a time and place for decadent, over-the-top dishes—and you'll find a few of these special fiesta meals in this cookbook. But the majority of recipes that make up the book will allow you to pair loads of colorful fruits and vegetables with healthy proteins for scrumptious meals you can enjoy every day.

As I traveled to other parts of these United States over the past years, I realized how difficult it was to find authentic Southwestern food. But I would often notice that the basic ingredients of the cuisine were available in many markets—so there was no reason that tasty, healthy Southwestern food couldn't be prepared anywhere, anytime. Luckily, the hard-to-find ingredients are fast becoming mainstream. Plus, if you can't find an ingredient at your local market, I've offered substitutes that will help you achieve comparable flavor results. Most ingredients are easy to acquire through the internet, as well.

While the inspiration for these recipes has been fueled by the pure beauty and nutrition of the regional flavors, some recipes come from traditional family meals, gathered over the years. Road trips around the region also played a big role in the creation of many dishes, while others have been prompted by the tastes and experiences from destinations across my home state like El Paso, Austin, San Antonio, and even tiny hole-in-the-wall locations that if you blinked, you'd miss! Journeys to Arizona, Oklahoma, New Mexico, and Colorado have also added to the book. I hope that these vibrant colors, earthy ingredients, and glorious aromas are reflected in this collection, and will make the flavors of Southwestern cuisine as mouth-watering to you as they are to me. *Alimentos frescos es buena comida!*

LINGO

No habla Espanol? No problemo. This list of translations and definitions will have you speaking like Sofia Vergara in no time.

A
Aqua de la Frutta – *an icy beverage made of blended fresh fruit and water*
Arroz – *rice*
Atole – *a cornflour drink*

B
Bunuelos – *a fritter*

C
Calabacitas – *squash*
Caldo – *broth*
Caliente – *hot*
Carne Asada – *grilled meat*
Carnitas – *little meats, typically fried or barbequed pork*
Ceviche – *raw seafood, marinated in citrus*
Chilaquiles – *crisp tortillas in chile sauce*
Chipotle – *smoked jalapeños*
Chorizo – *sausage*
Comal – *a smooth, flat griddle*

D
Dulce – *sweet*

E
Empanada – *a hand pie, a pastry*

F
Fideos – *noodles*
Flautas – *a flute*

H
Horchata – *a cold drink made with rice or nut milk*

L
Leche – *milk*

M
Manzana – *apple*
Michelada – *spicy cerveza, or beer*
Migas – *literally translates, "crumbs" and is a popular Mexican breakfast made with scrambled eggs and pieces of tortillas*
Mole – *literally translates, "mixture" and is a sauce, sometimes made with chocolate*

N
Naranja – *orange*

P
Papas – *potatoes*

Pepitas – *pumpkin seeds*
Pescado – *fish*
Pico de gallo – *a freshly made salsa*

Piloncillo sugar – *brown sugar made with sugar cane; often sold in the shape of a cone*
Pinon – *pine nut*
Pollo – *chicken*
Posole or Pozole – *corn/maize stew*

Q
Queso fresco – *fresh cheese*

S
Sopa – *soup*
Sopapilla – *puffed pillows of dough*

T
Tinga – *literally translates, "uproar"*
Torta – *a Mexican sandwich*
Tres Leches – *three milks*

V
Verde – *green*
Vino – *wine*

STALES

These are the basics you'll need in your pantry to help you create all the recipes in this cookbook.

Spices, nuts, seeds, and flavorings:

Coarse salt or sea salt
Black pepper corns
Ground cumin
Chili powder
Smoked paprika
Cone of piloncillo sugar
Dried Mexican oregano, or other
   oregano
Ground cinnamon
Canela sticks (Mexican cinnamon)
Onion powder
Garlic powder
Mexican vanilla, or other
   vanilla extract
Mexican Chocolate
Pumpkin seeds
Sesame seeds
Pine nuts
Hot sauce
Honey
Sesame oil
Almonds
Pecans

Fresh produce:

Tomatoes
Tomatillos
Jalapenos
Serranos
Assorted other chiles and bell
   peppers
Fresh fruit, such as limes, mangos,
pineapple, bananas, and apples
Onions, Spanish or other
Garlic
Potatoes
Fresh cilantro
Assorted squash
Haas Avocados
Cabbage
Lettuce
Corn on the cob
Carrots

Dried goods:

Dried beans – Anasazi, black, and
   pinto
Long grain white rice
Masa Harina
Corn husks
All-purpose flour
Yellow and blue cornmeal
Dried chile pods
Sugar
Brown sugar
Powdered sugar
Graham cracker crumbs

Dairy:

Cream
Butter
Cheeses: cream, cheddar, Longhorn,
   Asadero, pepper jack, colby jack
Milk

Meat, poultry, and seafood:

Beef brisket
Serrano ham
Pork tenderloins
Ground beef
Ground turkey
Chicken
Spanish Chorizo
Skirt steak
Tilapia
Shrimp
Pork shoulder
Bacon

Odds and ends:

Frozen corn, for those times when
   fresh is not available
Tortilla chips
Good quality prepackaged corn and
   flour tortillas, when time is factor
Olive oil
Vegetable oil and vegetable
   shortening
Good quality canned beans, when
   time is a factor
Vinegar
Sweetened flaked coconut
Canned, or frozen, hominy
Spanish olives
Black olives
Tomato paste
Sweetened condensed milk
Evaporated milk
Eggroll wrappers
Canned broth
Canned or frozen green chiles, but
   fresh roasted or frozen preferred

CONDIMENTOS

*Authentic sauces,
salsas, and tortillas*

PINT OF PICKLED PEPPERS

In the Southwest, this condiment is popular served with barbecue, Mexican food, or a bowl of pinto beans with cornbread on the side. As a kid, this was even on the table when we had fried chicken. It gives a kick to any dish! ★ *This spicy pepper mix is also known as* escabeche.

yields 1 pint

6 fresh jalapeño peppers, rinsed, stemmed, and cut into ½-inch rounds
1 carrot, peeled and cut into ¾-inch rounds
8 pearl onions, ends trimmed and peeled
3 cloves garlic, peeled and thinly sliced
¼ cup kosher salt
¼ cup Spanish olives
¼ cup white vinegar
¼ cup olive oil

Place the peppers, carrots, onions, and garlic into a medium mixing bowl and sprinkle with salt. Add just enough water to cover, and stir to distribute the salt. Cover the bowl with plastic wrap and refrigerate for 24 hours.

The next day, drain the water and rinse the ingredients in fresh water 2 times. Add the olives to the mix.

Whisk together the vinegar and oil, and pour over the pepper mix. Stir to evenly coat the mixture. Store in a tightly sealed pint jar, or serve immediately.

The pepper mix may be kept in a cool, dry place for up to 2 weeks, or refrigerated for up to 1 month.

NOTE: If refrigerated, the olive oil will thicken, so the mixture must be brought back to room temperature before serving.

GRILLED AVOCADO SALSA
WITH FRESH CORN TORTILLA CHIPS

The rich, smoky taste of Haas avocados (a large avocado, grown in our country and in Mexico) pairs perfectly with the other flavors of Southwestern cuisine. When Haas avocados are at their peak of ripeness they have a deep green exterior and the interior is smooth and creamy. ★ Grilled Avocado Salsa is a crowd favorite at my house—creamy avocado chunks with crisp, fresh corn, tastefully completed with tomatoes, onions and a delicious mix of seasonings. ★ Serve it as a dip with crispy Fresh Corn Tortilla Chips (recipe, p. 20), over a grilled steak, or atop steamed rice. It also works well as a condiment for tacos and tostadas.

yields 5 cups

3 medium Haas avocados, cut into
   halves with skin on, and pits removed
3 ears fresh corn, shucked and rinsed
½ medium red onion, peeled and diced
1 cup small grape tomatoes, halved
5 tablespoons olive oil, divided
2 tablespoons rice vinegar
1 ½ teaspoons chili powder
1 teaspoon cumin
¼ teaspoon salt
¼ teaspoon freshly ground
   black pepper

Prepare an outdoor grill, or preheat a grill pan on the stovetop over medium-high heat.

Place 2 tablespoons olive oil in a small dish. Brush the meat of the avocado halves with oil.

Brush the corncobs with the remaining oil in the dish. Place the corn on the grill or grill pan and char for 10 to 15 minutes, turning so that there is char on all sides. Set the corn aside to cool.

Place the avocado halves on the grill or grill pan cut side down, and heat 1 to 2 minutes, just long enough to create grill lines on the avocado.

Using a sharp knife, score the avocado halves into ½-inch cubes, being careful not to cut through the skins. Scoop the cubes out of the skins with a spoon and transfer to a medium mixing bowl.

Stand each ear of corn on one end to cut the kernels from the cob. Using a sharp knife, cut in a downward motion from top to bottom. Add the corn to the bowl with the avocado cubes. Fold in the tomato halves and diced onion.

In a separate bowl, whisk together the remaining 3 tablespoons olive oil, the rice vinegar, chili powder, cumin, salt, and pepper. Drizzle over the avocado mixture and gently stir to coat.

Scoop the salsa into a serving dish and serve immediately. This salsa may be refrigerated, covered, for 1 to 2 days, but squeeze a couple of teaspoons of lime juice over the top to preserve the color of the avocados.

FRESH CORN TORTILLA CHIPS

Making fresh corn tortilla chips is very simple and worth the little bit of labor it requires. This recipe works best using prepackaged tortillas to make the chips, which hold together better in the hot oil and are not as flaky as freshly made tortillas. ★ *Watch out, people make excuses to steal one or two each time they walk by the stove as you're cooking these! My suggestion is to place them on a baking sheet lined with paper towels as you remove them from the frying oil, then hide them in a warm oven until you are ready to serve!*

yields 4 dozen

1 dozen (6-inch) prepackaged corn
  tortillas
Vegetable oil for frying
Coarse salt
Juice of 1 lime, optional

Cut the tortillas into quarters.

Heat enough oil to reach a ¾-inch depth in a large skillet over medium heat. To test the hot oil, tear off a tiny piece of tortilla and toss it in the pan. When it sizzles, you are ready to fry the tortillas. Work in batches so you will not overcrowd the pan, and fry for about 2 minutes, turning to lightly brown each side, until crisp.

Use a slotted spoon or spatula to remove the tortillas from the oil, and transfer to paper towels to drain. Immediately sprinkle with salt as needed. Repeat the process until all the tortillas are fried.

When you are ready to serve, squeeze fresh lime juice over the chips, as desired.

Serve with Charred Salsa (recipe, p.41), Loaded Guacamole (recipe, p. 21), or Grilled Avocado Salsa (recipe, p. 18).

Corn tortilla chips will stay fresh in an airtight container for 2 days.

NOTE: Do not add the lime juice to the chips if you wish to store them.

LOADED GUACAMOLE

When it comes to guacamole, I'm a bit of a minimalist—a little salt, a little pepper, a squeeze of fresh lime, and you've got a tasty, healthy treat. But when special occasions call for something a little over the top, this one is loaded with extra flavor. ★ *Try it with a batch of Fresh Corn Tortilla Chips (recipe, p. 20).*

serves 4 to 6

2 large Haas avocados (choose ripe
   avocados that give a little when pressed)
2 slices bacon, cooked and crumbled
2 tablespoons diced tomato
2 tablespoons diced onion
3 tablespoons light sour cream
2 teaspoons light mayonnaise
2 tablespoons freshly squeezed lime juice
1 teaspoon fresh cilantro leaves, finely
   chopped
¼ teaspoon salt
¼ teaspoon black pepper
⅛ teaspoon crushed red pepper flakes,
   or substitute a dash of your choice
   hot sauce

Slice each avocado in half lengthwise, and remove the pits. Score each half with a knife, being careful not to cut into the skin, then slide the knife around the edges to release the avocado cubes. Scoop them out into a small bowl and mash with the tines of a fork. Stir in the bacon crumbles, tomato, and onion.

In another small bowl, whisk the remaining ingredients together; add to avocado mixture and stir to combine.

Place in a serving bowl and serve immediately with tortilla chips, or as a condiment with your favorite Southwestern food. Guacamole may be covered and refrigerated for up to 1 day.

Because the color will darken slightly, do not make this the day before you intend to serve it.

THREE AMIGOS PICO DE GALLO

Pico de Gallo is a mixture of tiny pieces of tomato, onion, and jalapeño that reflect the colors of the Mexican flag. The bright, fresh crunch is both cool and spicy at the same time. ★ *The trio not only tastes great on tacos and tostadas, it's great with steamed rice and wonderful as a dip for tortilla chips.*

yields about 1 cup

1 large tomato, peeled and finely diced
½ Spanish onion, peeled and finely diced
1 fresh jalapeño, stemmed, seeded, and finely diced
⅓ cup fresh cilantro leaves, roughly chopped
Juice of 1 lime
2 or 3 dashes of hot sauce, your choice brand
¼ teaspoon salt

Stir the tomato, onion, and jalapeño together in a serving bowl. Toss with the cilantro leaves, lime juice, hot sauce, and salt.

Serve chilled or at room temperature. Pico de Gallo may be refrigerated in an airtight container for up to 5 days.

MEXICAN CREMA WITH LIME

Crema is a slightly thinner version of sour cream, made with cream and an acid, such as vinegar or citrus juice. Only a small amount of crema is needed to enhance the flavor of any dish—from tacos and enchiladas to tostadas. ★ *It is a good substitute for recipes that call for sour cream. Cool, creamy, and smooth, Mexican Crema is a perfect partner for crunchy, spicy Southwestern dishes such as Chicken Tinga Tacos (recipe, p. 135) and Green Chile Beef Flautas (recipe, p. 46).*

yields 1 cup

½ pint heavy cream
1 tablespoon fresh lime juice
Zest of 1 lime
¼ teaspoon salt

Heat the cream in a small saucepan over low heat just enough to warm; the temperature should reach 95° to 100° F. Do not overheat.

Remove the pan from the stove and allow the cream to cool slightly. Whisk in the lime juice and pour into a lidded jar. Place the lid on the jar but do not screw it on tightly. Set the jar in a warm spot overnight, or up to 24 hours, until the crema begins to thicken.

When the crema thickens, stir in the lime zest and salt until well blended. Secure the lid and refrigerate the crema for 8 to 12 hours.

Crema will last, tightly sealed in the refrigerator, for up to 1 week.

BLUE CORN FLATBREAD

Flatbreads are popular in many shapes and sizes and have been around since man first began baking bread. There are lots of variations, and incorporating blue cornmeal gives this version a true American Indian flair. ★ Flatbreads are great for breakfast with Mango Jam (recipe, p. 34), or with butter and a steaming bowl of chili or soup.

yields 8

2 ¼ teaspoons active dry
    yeast (1 small packet)
2 ¼ cups bread flour, divided
½ cup blue cornmeal
1 teaspoon salt
3 tablespoons honey
1 tablespoon, plus 1 teaspoon
    vegetable oil

Pour 1 cup warm water (about 100° F) into the medium bowl of an electric mixer, sprinkle the dry yeast over the water, and allow it to dissolve. This should take about 1 minute.

In a separate bowl, stir together 2 cups flour, the cornmeal, and salt. With the electric mixer on low speed, slowly add the flour to the yeast mixture until the dough begins to come together. Add the honey and 1 tablespoon oil and mix until incorporated. If the dough is too wet or sticky, slowly incorporate the extra flour, up to ¼ cup, until you achieve the correct consistency.

When the dough pulls away from the sides of the mixer bowl, affix a dough hook and knead for 5 minutes. If you do not have a dough hook, turn the dough out onto a lightly floured surface and knead by hand for 5 minutes.

Rub 1 teaspoon oil over the top of the dough ball, cover with plastic wrap, and let the dough rest for 20 minutes.

Preheat the oven to 450° F.

If you have a pizza stone, which works well for baking flatbreads, place the stone in the oven to preheat. If not, line a flat baking sheet with parchment paper, or turn a baking sheet with sides over and line the top with parchment paper.

Divide the dough into 8 balls. Use your hands to pat each dough ball out to about a ¾-inch thickness.

Bake 2 to 4 flatbreads at a time, depending on the size of your baking sheet or stone. Bake for 2 to 3 minutes until slightly brown. Remove and stack the flatbreads atop each other. This allows the steam to escape, and the bread will flatten slightly.

Serve warm or at room temperature. Flatbread will keep in an airtight container for 5 days at room temperature, or in the refrigerator for up to 1 week. The flatbreads can be frozen and kept for up to 3 months. When you are ready to eat, thaw them at room temperature, and heat each separately for 15 seconds in a microwave.

PUMPKIN CORNBREAD

Pumpkin doesn't lend a pumpkin flavor to this recipe, but the pureed pumpkin adds moisture to the bread and really packs in extra nutrients. The texture is slightly dense and smooth, with crispy edges. Starting the cornbread on the stovetop in a cast iron skillet ensures you will get the crispy edges my Grandma Lightner always loved. ★ *If you enjoy baking pumpkin to make pumpkin puree, it will work beautifully in this recipe, but a quality canned pumpkin puree works well, too. Just be sure you pick up a puree and not a canned pie filling.* ★ *The subtle but classic Southwestern flavor pairs perfectly with soups, chiles, and stews.*

serves 8

Pumpkin Puree
1 small pie pumpkin

Cornbread
1 ½ cups yellow cornmeal
1 ½ cups all-purpose flour
1 tablespoon sugar
1 ½ tablespoons baking powder
1 ½ teaspoons salt
1 ½ cups milk
½ cup vegetable oil
2 large eggs
¾ cup prepared pumpkin puree, or
   substitute canned puree
1 tablespoon butter

To make the pumpkin puree, choose a small pie pumpkin. Clean the outside with a damp paper towel. Cut the pumpkin in half from end to end with sharp knife, and remove the seeds, membranes, and strings. (TIP: I like to clean the seeds and toast them on a baking sheet with a drizzle of olive oil and some sea salt for healthy snack. Toast them at 375° F for 1 hour, stirring every 15 minutes.)

Brush the interior of the pumpkin halves with 1 tablespoon vegetable oil, and place the halves cut-side down on a baking sheet lined with parchment paper. Bake for 45 minutes in a preheated 350° F oven. Allow to cool, then scoop the flesh out and transfer to a blender. The outer skin will be soft and separate easily from the flesh; discard the outer skin. Puree the pumpkin in the blender on low speed for 1 minute, or until smooth.

In a large mixing bowl, combine the cornmeal, flour, sugar, baking powder, and salt. Whisk the milk, oil, and eggs into the dry ingredients, then whisk in the pumpkin puree until the batter is smooth.

Preheat oven to 400° F.

Heat the butter in a cast-iron skillet over medium heat. Pour the batter into the skillet and cook for 1 minute, then transfer to the preheated oven and bake, uncovered, for 20 to 25 minutes, or until a toothpick inserted in the center comes out clean.

Slice and serve hot with additional butter, as desired.

Leftover cornbread may be covered in plastic wrap and refrigerated for up to 1 week. Reheat in a microwave, approximately 15 seconds per serving.

HANDMADE CORN TORTILLAS

Like flour tortillas, the basics for corn tortillas are quite simple. Corn tortillas will flatten easily in a tortilla press, but a rolling pin may also be used. Handmade corn tortillas are crisp, yet tender, and they are the ultimate vessel for freshly made tacos. The aroma is pure Southwest! ★

yields 1 dozen

2 cups masa harina, found in most supermarkets near the all-purpose flour

In a medium mixing bowl, combine the masa harina with 1 ½ cups warm water, stirring with a spoon. Knead with your hands until the dough has a smooth consistency. Cover the bowl with a kitchen towel and let the dough rest for 15 minutes.

Preheat a comal, griddle, or cast-iron skillet over medium heat for 10 to 15 minutes.

Divide the dough into 12 balls. Working with one ball at a time, press the dough between two 8- to 10-inch sheets of wax paper, and use a rolling pin to roll the dough out to a 5 ½- to 6-inch diameter disk.

If you are using a tortilla press, cut 2 pieces of plastic about the width of the tortilla press. (For a sturdy, reusable plastic, I cut a zip-top freezer bag apart to use in place of plastic wrap.) Lay one piece of plastic onto the bottom plate of the press. Place a dough ball in the center of the plastic, and top with a second sheet of plastic. Close the top of the press and apply a slight amount of pressure to the lever. Open the press.

Peel off the top sheet of wax paper or plastic and lift the tortilla with the bottom sheet attached. Place the tortilla facedown on your palm and gently peel off the bottom sheet of wax paper or plastic with you other hand. Place the tortilla onto the dry, heated pan.

Cook one side of each tortilla for about 30 seconds or until the edges begin to dry. Flip over with a spatula and cook the other side for 15 to 30 seconds. To allow the tortilla to puff up, adding a layer of air, flip the tortilla over again and briefly press down on the center with a spatula. Remove the tortilla from the heat and place in foil to keep warm until you are ready to serve. Repeat the process for each dough ball.

NOTE: For a tortilla with crispy edges, do not stack them until cool or they will create steam and lose their crispness.

Leftover corn tortillas may be kept, refrigerated, in plastic wrap or a plastic bag for 2 to 3 days. Reheat on a dry skillet for 1 or 2 minutes on each side. Or for a soft corn tortilla, heat in the microwave for about 10 seconds per tortilla.

1. Add warm water to masa harina   2. Stir with a spoon, then knead the dough with your hand   3. Shape dough into a ball and divide into 12 balls

4. Place a piece of plastic or wax paper on the tortilla press   5. Put 1 ball in the center of the plastic   6. Layer another piece of plastic on top of the dough ball

7. Press down on the tortilla press   8. Open and peel off the top piece of plastic   9. Lay the tortilla on one hand and remove bottom piece of plastic

HANDMADE FLOUR TORTILLAS

Flour tortillas are used to make burritos and are an option for soft tacos. Nothing beats any meal accompanied with a warm flour tortilla. There are a few basic ways to make flour tortillas, but I find that the technique is as important as the recipe. ★ *Flour tortillas are made by rolling the dough out with a rolling pin to achieve a thin tortilla. Due to the gluten in all-purpose flour, they tend to "spring" back, or puff up slightly, when using a tortilla press, the traditional way to prepare corn tortillas. Cake flour has less gluten, so substitute it for all-purpose flour if you desire a thin tortilla when using a tortilla press.*

yields 8

2 cups all-purpose flour
1 teaspoon baking powder
1 teaspoon salt
3 tablespoons shortening

In a medium mixing bowl, stir together the flour, baking powder, and salt. Cut in the shortening using your hands. Add hot water a little at a time, up to ¾ cup, stirring to incorporate, until you reach a smooth consistency, being careful that the dough does not become too sticky.

Turn the dough out onto a floured surface and knead for 2 minutes. Let the dough rest for about 15 minutes, then divide it into 8 balls. Let the dough balls rest for another 4 to 5 minutes.

Preheat a griddle, comal, or cast-iron skillet over medium heat for 2 to 3 minutes while you roll out the dough.

Dust a rolling pin with flour and roll out each ball to 7 to 8 inches in diameter.

Over medium heat, cook each tortilla individually on the dry, preheated pan. When bubbles start to form, continue cooking for 30 seconds, then flip the tortilla over and cook another 30 seconds. When the tortilla is done, wrap in aluminum foil and place in a 200° F oven to keep them warm. Repeat the process for each tortilla.

Leftover tortillas may be kept, refrigerated, in plastic wrap or a plastic bag for up to 1 week. Reheat on a dry skillet for 1 or 2 minutes on each side. Or for a soft flour tortilla, heat in the microwave for about 10 seconds per tortilla. If you microwave multiple soft tortillas, place a damp paper towel between each one and microwave at 10 second intervals.

TIP: Depending on the altitude, if your flour tortillas do not begin to bubble while cooking, make the next batch using an additional ¼ to ½ teaspoon baking powder. Or if they tend to get tough after a couple of hours, try adding 1 additional tablespoon of shortening to your next batch.

Tortilla Press Method

Substitute cake flour for the all-purpose flour; otherwise all ingredients are the same.

Cut two pieces of plastic wrap the width of your tortilla press. (For a sturdy, reusable plastic, I like to cut zip-top freezer bags apart to use in place of plastic wrap.) Lay one piece of plastic onto the bottom plate of the press and spray the plastic lightly with non-stick cooking spray. Flatten a dough ball into a disk between your palms and place the dough in the center of the press, or slightly higher. Spray the other sheet of plastic with non-stick cooking spray and place that on top of the dough.

Close the press and apply slight pressure to the handle to flatten the dough. Open the press and check to see if the tortilla has spread to approximately 8 inches in diameter. If needed, press again, using more pressure to achieve the correct size. To remove, peel off the top sheet of plastic, and lift the tortilla from the press using the bottom sheet of plastic. Place the tortilla on your palm and gently peel the plastic back. Repeat the process to cook each tortilla, according to the directions.

EL PESTO

If you're like me, you often wind up with leftover fresh herbs, and nuts or seeds. This Southwestern-style pesto is the perfect answer to a light sauce for grilled chicken or fish, or a dressing to serve over steamed rice. It's also a great condiment to use with any taco or tostada. ★ *Try it on Blackened Chicken Tacos, (recipe p. 116).*

yields 3 cups

4 fresh jalapeños, stemmed and seeded
¼ cup shelled pumpkin seeds, or pinion
   (pine) nuts, or a combination of both
4 cloves garlic, peeled
2 ½ cups fresh cilantro leaves
2 ½ cups fresh flat-leaf parsley leaves
½ teaspoon salt
½ teaspoon black pepper
¾ cup olive oil
½ cup grated Parmesan cheese

Place the first 7 ingredients in a blender and blend on medium speed until the mixture has a smooth consistency, but not yet pureed. With the blender on low speed, slowly drizzle in the olive oil through the small opening in the blender lid. Add the Parmesan and continue to blend until well incorporated.

Serve immediately, or refrigerate leftovers in an airtight container for up to 1 week. Allow the pesto to return to room temperature before serving.

TIP: Smash the garlic cloves with the flat side of a broad knife blade and the peel will slip right off.

QUESO FRESCO
(FRESH CHEESE)

If you've never made cheese, this is the one to begin with, and the only special equipment you need is a cheesecloth. Queso Fresco is fundamental in the cheese-making world, employing simple ingredients and a simple technique. It's made from cow's milk and is a classic Mexican/Latin American topping to crumble on salads, tacos, tostadas, and other dishes. ★ *Queso Fresco can also be chilled and sliced, but is not necessarily a melting cheese. It is similar to feta cheese, and sometimes known as farmer's cheese, or queso blanco (white cheese). Queso Fresco provides a light, tangy taste atop anything from fresh salads to heavier dishes.*

yields about 6 ounces

4 cups whole cow's milk, or organic
   whole milk
1 tablespoon kosher salt
1 tablespoon white vinegar
2 teaspoons freshly squeezed lime juice
Lime zest

In a medium saucepan, bring the milk and salt to a boil over medium-high heat. Reduce the heat to low and stir in the vinegar and lime juice. Curds will start to form almost immediately and will separate from the whey. When this happens, remove the pan from the heat. The curds are finished forming at this point in the process.

Line a colander with cheesecloth and strain the mixture to catch the curds. Let the cheese drain for 15 minutes, then gather the sides of the cheesecloth up to completely cover the curds and twist to remove any excess water/whey.

For a drier cheese, tie the sides of the cheesecloth to a long wooden spoon or dowel, place the spoon across the top of an empty bowl or pan, and let the cheese curds drain for up to 2 additional hours.

The cheese is ready to crumble as soon as the whey has drained. Sprinkle with lime zest and taste to see if you need any additional salt. Crumble and serve immediately, or refrigerate in an airtight container for up to 3 days.

1. Place milk and salt into a saucepan

2. After boiling, curds will begin to form

3. Strain the whey through the cheesecloth

4. Squeeze the cheesecloth to remove whey

5. Tie the cheesecloth around a spoon handle

6. Give the cheesecloth one more tight squeeze

7. Remove the cheesecloth

8. Sprinle with lime zest and additional salt

9. Crumble and serve atop tacos, salads, etc.

MANGO JAM

This method for making jam can be made without pectin as a thickener. And with only three simple ingredients, it's a snap to make. You'll have fresh, homemade jam within an hour or so. It's delicious on toast for breakfast, or shortbread biscuits for dessert. Try it with warm Blue Corn Flatbread (recipe, p. 24). ★

yields 2 pints

4 ½ cups fresh cubed mango
1 cup sugar
3 tablespoons lemon juice

Rinse the mangos. Note that there is a long, slender pit in the middle of the mango. Carefully slice the mangos into halves lengthwise, leaving about ½-inch down the center to avoid the pit. Score each mango, as demonstrated, and cut the cubes of mango from each half and place in a medium saucepan.

Add the sugar and lemon juice to the saucepan, stirring to combine. Let it rest for 20 minutes. Then, cook over medium heat, stirring occasionally, for 20 minutes, or until the temperature of the jam reaches 220° F on a candy/deep fry thermometer.

In the meantime, fill a stockpot or canner approximately ⅔ full of water. Bring to a boil over high heat, then reduce the heat to medium-high. Place the jars and lids (rings and flats) into the hot water bath for about 10 minutes to sterilize them. Use tongs to remove the sterilized items from the water and transfer them to clean kitchen towels to dry.

Pour the hot jam mixture into the jars. Place the flats on the jars and screw on the rings.

If you are planning to use the jam right away—or within 7 to 10 days—simply refrigerate. If not, process the sealed jam jars by placing them in a pot of boiling water over medium-high heat for 10 minutes. Remove the jars from the water and set them upside-down onto kitchen towels to seal the lid and to cool. The jars of jam will keep up to a year in a cool, dry place. Refrigerate when opened.

Cubing a Mango

Cut the mango in half down each side of the seed, then hold the mango in the cup of your hand and score each half with a paring knife. Place your thumbs on each side of the skin, press up to invert the mango. Slice the cubes of mango from the skin.

RED CHILE

Red Chile is the base for many traditional Southwestern dishes. This versatile sauce is used for Stacked Enchiladas (recipe, p. 108). It can also go into casseroles or be used with huevos rancheros. ★

yields about 2 cups

12 dried chile pods, such as New Mexico
   or Guajillo chiles
2 cups water or stock
1 teaspoon salt
3 cloves garlic, peeled
1 teaspoon cumin
1 tablespoon olive oil

Clean the chile pods with a damp paper towel. Remove the stems with a paring knife. Split the pods horizontally with the knife and remove the seeds.

Heat a cast-iron skillet over medium heat. Flatten the pods and place them in the hot skillet to toast for a few seconds until aromatic. Work in batches until all the pods are toasted.

Place the pods in a stockpot and add enough water to cover. Bring the pot to a boil over high heat, then reduce the heat to medium-low and simmer, uncovered, for 30 minutes.

Remove from heat and let the chiles cool in the cooking liquid, then discard the liquid. Transfer the chile pods to a blender along with 2 cups water, or stock. Add the salt, garlic, and cumin, and blend on high until smooth. Use care: if the cooking liquid is still a little warm, it can form pressure inside the blender causing the liquid to splatter over the top.

Strain the mixture through a mesh sieve over a saucepan or a glass bowl (plastic will stain).

Heat the oil in a skillet over medium heat, add the sauce and cook for 15 minutes, until it has reduced and thickens.

Use immediately or refrigerate in a glass jar with a lid for up to 1 week. Red Chile can also be kept frozen in a freezer bag for up to 3 months. When you are ready to use, thaw at room temperature, and reheat 3 to 5 minutes in a skillet over medium heat.

THE RED CHILE 12-STEP PROGRAM

1. If chiles are very dry, cover cleaned chiles with boiling water to soften for a couple of minutes. Some will be very pliable and this step will not be necessary

2. Remove stems from chiles

3. Cut chiles open, vertically, and remove seeds

4. Lay chiles flat in a cast iron skillet

5. Working in batches, toast chiles for a few seconds on both sides, then place toasted chiles in a stockpot, cover with water, and bring to a boil (not shown in photos). Reduce heat to medium-low and simmer for 30 minutes. Let cool, slightly, in cooking liquid

6. Crush garlic and remove skins

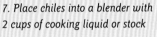

7. Place chiles into a blender with 2 cups of cooking liquid or stock

8. Add garlic, salt, and cumin to blender

9. Blend on medium speed until well combined

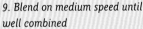

10. Pour mixture through a strainer over a bowl or saucepan

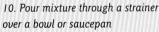

11. Press mixture through the strainer with the back of a spoon

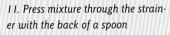

12. Sauce is now ready to add to 1 tablespoon oil in a saucepan over medium heat to reduce and thicken

ROASTED GREEN CHILE PEPPERS

People in the Wild West were and are still very opinionated about their green chile. But one thing we all agree on: how to roast green chiles. ★ *New Mexico, Anaheim, and Big Jim are all green chile varieties that roast well. Markets typically sell both mild and hot versions. You can roast just a few, or batches of 12 or more. I often roast an entire case at a time to freeze for use in the year ahead.*

1 dozen or more New Mexico (Hatch), Anaheim, or Big Jim green chiles

There are 3 roasting options.

1. In the Oven
Preheat the oven to 425° F. Place whole chiles directly on an oven rack, positioned 6 inches below the broiler.

2. On a Grill
Using a gas grill set to medium heat, or a prepared charcoal grill, place the chiles directly on a grate set approximately 6 inches above the heat source.

3. On the Stovetop
Cook on a gas stovetop on medium heat. Roast 1 or 2 chiles at a time, using tongs to hold them 1 to 2 inches above the flame.

For each of these methods, roast the chiles on one side until the skin is charred and blistered, 3 to 5 minutes. About 75% of the skin will bubble into blisters. Use tongs to turn the chiles and char and blister the other side for 3 to 5 minutes.

Place the chiles in a glass bowl and cover with plastic wrap. Let them cool for about 15 minutes. This will allow the chiles to steam and will loosen the charred and blistered skins. Remove and discard the skins and stems.

The chiles are now ready to use. They can be stuffed whole to make chile rellenos, cut open and used whole on sandwiches and burgers, or diced to use in sauces, rice dishes, and casseroles.

To store, let the chiles cool completely, then place them in 1-quart zip-top freezer bags, or dice and divide into ½-cup airtight containers.

Chiles may be refrigerated in tightly sealed containers for up to 1 week, or frozen for up to 1 year. Thaw and use as needed.

WESTERN GREEN CHILE

Some recipes contain beef, others incorporate pork. But this recipe is the perfect base to go with any meal. ★ *We eat green chile for breakfast, lunch, and dinner. It is the ideal condiment to jazz potatoes or rice. It's also great with steak, and makes for the tastiest Green Chile Chicken Enchiladas (recipe, p. 110).*

yields 2 cups

1 dozen roasted Hatch, Anaheim, or Big Jim chile peppers (recipe, p. 38, or use pre-roasted), stemmed, seeded, and diced
1 tablespoon olive oil
½ medium Spanish onion, diced
1 small tomato, diced
1 clove garlic, peeled and minced
1 tablespoon all-purpose flour
1 cup beef or chicken stock
¼ teaspoon ground cumin
¼ teaspoon salt

Heat the oil in a medium skillet over medium heat. Sauté the diced onion 2 to 3 minutes, until translucent. Add the diced chiles, tomato, and garlic and continue to sauté for an additional 1 to 2 minutes. Whisk in the flour until smooth. Add the stock and continue whisking. Stir in the cumin and salt. Reduce the heat to medium-low, cover, and simmer for 30 minutes, stirring occasionally.

Serve warm. Green chile may be refrigerated in an airtight container for up to 1 week. To reheat, place in a small saucepan, stir in 1 or 2 tablespoons of water, and cook over medium heat for 4 or 5 minutes until heated through.

RED CHILE SAUCE

Red Chile Sauce is similar to Red Chile, but instead of making a puree from the dried chile pods, this one is made with ground chile powder. I typically purchase the chiles already ground. This gravy can be used in a variety of Mexican casseroles, and with rolled enchiladas. ★ *It can be used to thicken posole, and is the braising liquid for Jacqueline's Chile Braised Beef (recipe, p.133).*

yields 1 ½ cups

2 tablespoons vegetable shortening
3 tablespoons all-purpose flour
½ cup chile powder
¼ teaspoon oregano
¼ teaspoon cumin
Salt, to taste

In a medium skillet over medium heat, melt the shortening. Add the flour and stir until the mixture is golden in color. Reduce the heat to medium-low and whisk in the chile powder, being careful that roux does not brown or burn, or it will taste bitter. Whisk in 2 cups water. Stir in the oregano and cumin and reduce the heat to medium-low. Continue cooking for 15 minutes, stirring often. Add salt to taste.

NOTE: The amount of chili, or chile powder may be reduced to 1/3 cup for a less intense flavor. Alternatively, beef or chicken broth may be used in place of water for a different flavor.

Use immediately, or refrigerate for up to 1 week in an airtight container. When reheating, whisk in a tablespoon or so of water, then cook over medium heat for 3 to 5 minutes in a skillet or saucepan.

CHARRED SALSA

My sister-in-law will whip up a batch of tomato salsa to serve at most family functions, either as a condiment with our meal or served with tortilla chips as a snack. A classic Mexican salsa blends fresh tomatoes, jalapeños, and salt for a taste we love. And for something a little different, this smoky charred version has a deep, rich flavor that pairs well with meat dishes, too. Charred salsa is great with Green Chile Beef Flautas (recipe, p. 46). ★ If you prefer a salsa with less heat, use gloved hands to cut open the charred peppers and discard the seeds and membranes before placing the peppers in the food processor.

yields 1 ½ cups

6 large Roma tomatoes
1 Spanish onion, peeled and halved
1 jalapeño pepper
1 serrano pepper
Juice of 1 lime
½ teaspoon garlic powder
½ teaspoon salt

Heat an outdoor grill to medium-high, or an oven to 425° F.

Place the tomatoes, onion halves, and the peppers onto the grill over medium-high heat, or on a baking sheet in the preheated oven. Char for approximately 10 to 15 minutes, turning halfway through, or until the outer skins begin to brown and blister. Remove from heat and set aside to cool.

When they are cool enough to handle, remove the stems from the peppers. Place the tomatoes, onion, and peppers into a food processor, and add the lime juice, garlic powder, and salt. Pulse until the salsa consists of small uniform chunks.

Serve with tortilla chips, or drizzle over your favorite Southwestern food. Salsa can be refrigerated for up to 5 days in an airtight container; the heat will intensify the longer it rests.

SMOKY CHIPOTLE BARBECUE SAUCE

PaPaw Dub's beef brisket, smoked with mesquite wood and drizzled with his homemade barbecue sauce, will always be one of my favorite meals. When we were young, PaPaw Dub got my brother, Mike, up early one morning to load the wood box on the smoker with mesquite wood. Mike started to fill it with several pieces of wood, the way PaPaw instructed him, but he decided to cram the thing plum full, all the way to the brim so he wouldn't have to keep adding wood later—not a good idea. PaPaw came out and lit the wood . . . then, POOF! As they stood in complete silence my brother began snickering and giggling and staring at PaPaw's face. Finally, PaPaw said, "What!?" Mike meekly informed him when he lit the wood, it singed his eyebrows clean off! I won't mention what PaPaw Dub said next. ★ I'm sure there were many times we should have listened better, and we definitely should have paid better attention to how PaPaw made his award-winning briskets. But we did get the barbecue sauce recipe right. Over the years, we have taken his recipe and added certain flavors to suit the meal we are preparing. This barbecue sauce marries up with Mesquite Smoked Brisket (recipe, p.96) to create an unforgettable meal. ★ Cook and prepare meat dishes using as much or as little of the sauce as you like, or serve the sauce on the side. This recipe may be halved if you don't need much sauce, but every time I do that I dance around the kitchen eating it by the spoonful, wishing I had made a full batch.

yields 2 cups

3 (4-ounce) cans tomato paste
½ cup cola (regular, not diet)
¼ cup white vinegar
½ cup light corn syrup
½ cup dark brown sugar
2 tablespoons chipotle-adobo paste, or
 canned chipotles in adobo sauce,
 finely minced
2 tablespoons freshly squeezed orange
 juice
2 tablespoons Worcestershire sauce
2 tablespoons soy sauce
2 teaspoons salt
2 teaspoons freshly ground black pepper
1 teaspoon freshly grated ginger root
½ teaspoon onion powder
½ teaspoon garlic powder

Whisk all the ingredients together in a medium saucepan with ½ cup water. Cook over medium heat until the sauce comes just to a boil, then reduce the heat to low and simmer for 20 minutes, stirring often.

Remove the pan from the heat, cover, and allow to cool to room temperature. The sauce will thicken as it cools. It may be refrigerated for up to 1 week in an airtight container. Reheat in a saucepan over medium heat for 3 to 5 minutes.

NOTE: When you purchase a can of chipotle chiles in adobo sauce and only intend to use a little, throw them in the blender for a couple of good turns. Spoon the mixture into an ice cube tray, freeze, then pop out the frozen chile cubes and place them in a zip-top freezer bag to store. Take out one cube at a time to add to sauces and other recipes as needed. A standard ice cube will be about 2 tablespoons.

SIZZLING SNACKS & APPETIZERS

Way beyond tortilla chips and salsa

GREEN CHILE BEEF FLAUTAS

A slow-cooker renders the most tender, juicy beef to use for shredded beef tacos, and it's the method I like to use to cook the filling for flautas. ★ *If you don't have the Western Green Chile at hand, you may substitute 2 cups frozen, diced green chiles, or a good jar of store-bought green chile salsa. I've used both in a pinch.*

serves 6 to 8

3 pounds rump roast
I teaspoon salt
I teaspoon black pepper
2 cups Western Green Chile, (recipe,
    p. 39)
Vegetable oil, for frying
18 prepackaged corn tortillas

Place I cup water into a slow-cooker. Season the roast with salt and pepper on both sides, place it in the slow-cooker, and pour 2 cups Western Green Chile over the meat. Cover and cook for 8 hours on low heat.

Shred the cooked roast using two forks and set aside in a bowl.

Heat enough oil to reach a I-inch depth in a deep skillet, or other pan suitable for frying, over medium heat.

Dip the tortillas one at a time into the oil for I or 2 seconds, to make the tortilla more flexible for rolling. Place the tortillas on a paper towel-lined plate and fill each one with about 3 tablespoons shredded beef. Roll into a cylinder and secure each flauta with a couple of toothpicks. This will keep them from unrolling during the frying.

Before frying the first flauta, check the heat of the oil by placing a small piece of beef or tortilla into the oil. If it sizzles, the oil is ready. Using tongs, place I or 2 flautas at a time into the hot oil, and cook 2 to 3 minutes on each side, until golden brown. When you remove the flautas from the oil with the tongs, tilt the flautas over the skillet to drain excess oil from the tortilla into the skillet (instead of onto your plate).

Place the fried flautas on a paper towel-lined plate.

Serve warm and pass your choice of topping or salsa, such as Mexican Crema with Lime (recipe, p. 23), or Charred Salsa (recipe, p. 41).

Leftovers may be refrigerated in an airtight container for up to I week. Reheat the flautas on a baking sheet in a 350° F oven for about I5 minutes.

CHEDDAR NICKELS CALIENTE

These crackers are delightfully thin and crisp, and packed with flavor. This recipe was inspired by the classic cheese straws, which are commonly served at parties in the South. When I was a young bride I didn't have the necessary equipment to make cheese straws, which requires a pastry bag and star tip. So, I would roll the dough into logs, chill it, and slice it into crackers. ★ This recipe is the caliente, or hot, version of my cheddar crackers and can be enjoyed with dips or small bites at parties.

yields 9 dozen

1 ½ cups all-purpose flour
½ teaspoon salt
½ teaspoon cayenne
1 (8-ounce) block cheddar cheese, grated
½ cup (1 stick) unsalted butter, room
    temperature
1 fresh jalapeño, stemmed, seeded,
    and finely diced

In a medium mixing bowl, combine the flour, salt, and cayenne.

With an electric mixer, or a food processor equipped with a stainless steel mixing blade, cream the cheese and butter until well blended. Gradually add the flour mixture until it is fully incorporated. It will seem as though the dough will not come together, but when you press it together with your fingertips it should hold its shape.

Dump the dough onto a large piece of wax paper. Add the diced jalapeño and work it into the dough as you shape the dough into a log.

Divide the dough log in half and use your hands to roll each piece into a 1-inch diameter log, about 8-inches long. Wrap the logs in wax paper and refrigerate for 1 to 2 hours, or you may make these a day or so ahead of time and refrigerate until ready to cook. (If the dough has been refrigerated for a day or more, let it rest at room temperature for 15 minutes before slicing.)

Preheat the oven to 350° F.

Slice the dough logs into ¼-to ⅛-inch thick rounds. Place the rounds on baking sheets lined with parchment paper, and bake for 18 to 20 minutes. Allow the crackers to cool completely before serving. These crackers will keep in an airtight container at room temperature for up to 2 weeks.

NOTE: The cheese may be grated using the grating blade of the food processor before switching to the mixing blade. If you do not have a food processor or electric mixer, the dough may be kneaded by hand. The heat of your hands will help to bring the mixture together and form the dough. When there's a will there's a way!

TEX-MEX POTATO SKINS

When you're looking for a hearty, healthy snack food for your next get-together, try these great tasting potato skins, made without frying. To turn these potato skins into a main dish, add a layer of Texas Beef and Bean Chili (recipe, p. 72) in the final step. ★

serves 10 to 12

2 pounds small Yukon Gold potatoes, scrubbed and dried
2 tablespoons olive oil
Kosher salt
1 cup grated Longhorn, or cheddar cheese
1 tomato, diced
¼ cup pickled jalapeño slices
4 green onions, thinly sliced
⅓ cup sliced black olives

Optional toppings
Light sour cream, or Mexican Crema with Lime (recipe, p. 23)
Charred Salsa (recipe, p. 41)
Hot sauce, to taste

Preheat the oven to 425° F.

Pierce the skin of each potato 2 or 3 times with a fork, place them on a baking sheet, and bake for 30 minutes. Test the potatoes with a fork to see if they are tender; depending on the size of the potatoes, you may need to cook them longer. When they are done, set the baking sheet aside to cool slightly. Do not turn the oven off.

When they have cooled enough to handle, cut the potatoes in half lengthwise. Scoop out part of the potato from each half (reserve it for another use or discard), leaving a ¼- to ½-inch of baked potato lining the skin. Brush the potatoes on all sides lightly with olive oil, and place back on the baking sheet, cut-side down. Sprinkle with coarse salt and bake the potatoes for 20 minutes more, or until the cut edges begin to brown and get crispy. Remove the potatoes from the oven. Turn them over, sprinkle the grated cheese inside each potato, and place under the broiler for 1 to 2 minutes until the cheese is melted.

Layer the tomato, jalapeños, onions, and olives in each potato skin and serve warm with toppings of your choice. Leftovers may be refrigerated in an airtight container, minus the fresh toppings, for up to 1 week. Reheat the potato skins in a preheated 425° oven for 10 to 15 minutes.

SHRIMP CEVICHE SHOOTERS

Ceviche is the Spanish word for a fresh seafood dish cooked in an acidic liquid, such as citrus juice or vinegar. Typically, this recipe is made with lime and raw fish, such as red snapper, or with shrimp. The acid reacts with the protein in the seafood and "cooks" it. Salt, peppers, and other spices can be added. ★ *I like to serve this as an appetizer in little shot glasses, with a wooden pick or small seafood fork.*

yields 12 small bites, or 6 appetizers

½ pound shrimp, peeled and deveined
1 to 2 fresh limes
¼ teaspoon salt
½ red bell pepper, stemmed, seeded,
  and diced
½ yellow bell pepper, stemmed, seeded,
  and diced
3 tablespoons fresh cilantro leaves

Rinse the shrimp in cold water and pat dry. Cut them into ½- to ¾-inch pieces and place in a shallow bowl. Squeeze enough lime juice over the shrimp to completely cover, and let them rest for at least 20 minutes. The "cooking" process is complete once the shrimp turns pink and opaque. I prefer to let the lime juice "cook" the shrimp for 35 or 40 minutes, but after 20 minutes, test every 5 to 10 minutes to make sure the texture does not become tough.

Once the shrimp is ready, stir together with the salt, diced bell peppers, and fresh cilantro. Spoon the ceviche into shot glasses (or tasting spoons). Top with an additional squeeze of lime juice and more cilantro leaves, as desired.

GULF OF MEXICO SUSHI ROLLS

Borrowing a term from Asian cuisine, sushi, or rolls of rice, is a great way to show off this combination of flavors. It's a fusion of East meets Southwest. ★

serves 6

1 cup cooked black beans (recipe, p. 93), or canned black beans, drained and rinsed

¾ cup uncooked medium grain, or sushi rice

2 tablespoons fresh lime juice, divided

1 Haas avocado

1 tablespoon olive oil

½ pound small to medium shrimp, peeled and deveined

¼ teaspoon crushed red pepper flakes

⅛ teaspoon salt

2 (10-inch) flour tortillas

Optional toppings

Light sour cream

Hot sauce, your choice brand

Mexican Crema with Lime (recipe, p. 23)

Heat the black beans in a small saucepan over medium heat for 3 or 4 minutes, until warm. Mash them using a handheld potato masher, until the beans are spreadably smooth, but still retain a little texture.

Prepare the rice per package instructions, then set aside to cool to room temperature, and drizzle with 1 tablespoon lime juice.

Cut the avocado in half lengthwise and remove the pit. Using a paring knife, run the tip of the knife between the meat of the avocado and the skin to loosen each half. Using a tablespoon, gently scoop out the avocado halves. Place the avocado halves cut-side down onto a cutting board and dice them into ½-inch cubes. Squeeze 1 tablespoon of lime juice over the diced avocado to help preserve the color.

Heat the olive oil in a skillet over medium-high heat and add the shrimp. Season with red pepper flakes and salt, and sauté for 3 to 4 minutes, stirring frequently, until the shrimp turn pink and opaque. Remove and set the shrimp aside to cool slightly. When they have cooled, dice them into ¼- to ½-inch pieces.

Place the tortillas on a clean cutting board. Spread ½ cup mashed black beans into a thin, even layer over each tortilla. Next, evenly spread the rice atop the layer of black beans. Place an equal amount of avocado onto each tortilla, then add a layer of diced shrimp onto each. Use the bottom of a dry measuring cup or small skillet to tamp down the layers as you go.

Using your fingertips, or a bamboo sushi roller, roll the tortilla up like a jellyroll. Trim the ends to create a smooth, even edge, and cut into 1-inch pieces. Repeat the process with the other tortilla. If the black bean paste and rice don't hold the rolls together, use a toothpick to secure the tortilla. (In the photo, the decorative toothpicks are an easy way for guests to pick up and secure the sushi roll.) Serve with your choice of optional toppings.

Gulf Coast Sushi Rolls can be served at room temperature, or refrigerated and served chilled. Leftovers may be refrigerated in an airtight container for up to 2 days.

SPICY SWEET PECANS

Spicy Sweet Pecans are a treat for any occasion. Your friends and family will think you've been to one of those expensive candied nut shops, and they'll love the little kick of cayenne. ★ *This recipe makes an excellent holiday gift, packaged in a cellophane bag or a colorful mason jar, and tied with a pretty bow.*

yields 1 pound

4 tablespoons unsalted butter

4 tablespoons light corn syrup

2 tablespoons grated piloncillo sugar,
   or brown sugar

1 teaspoon cinnamon

½ teaspoon Mexican vanilla,
   or other vanilla extract

½ teaspoon salt

¼ teaspoon cayenne

1 pound pecan halves

Preheat the oven to 250° F.

In a medium saucepan, melt the butter over medium heat. Stir in the corn syrup, sugar, cinnamon, vanilla extract, salt, and cayenne. Continue cooking for 1 to 2 minutes, until the sugar is dissolved. Then remove from the heat.

Add the pecans to the saucepan, stirring to coat, and pour the mixture out onto a baking sheet lined with parchment paper.

Bake in preheated oven for 1 hour, stirring every 15 minutes. Spicy Sweet Pecans may be refrigerated in an airtight container for 3 to 4 weeks (if they last that long).

TOSTADAS
WITH SHRIMP AND GUACAMOLE

Tostadas are made with crispy corn tortillas, and are as popular in the Southwest as crackers and cheese. Make them small to serve as an appetizer and offer an array of ingredients as toppings. ★ *Tostada shells can also be made by frying store-bought corn tortillas the same way Fresh Corn Tortilla Chips (recipe p. 20) are made.*

serves 6

Tostada Shell
2 cups masa harina, found in most
    supermarkets near the all-purpose
    flour
½ cup vegetable oil

Topping
1 tablespoon olive oil
½ pound medium shrimp,
    peeled and deveined
1 jalapeño, stemmed, seeded, and
    finely diced
½ teaspoon salt, divided
¼ teaspoon ground black pepper,
    divided
1 Haas avocado
2 teaspoons fresh lime juice

In a medium mixing bowl, use a fork to stir the masa harina together with 1 ½ cups warm water. Knead the dough with your hands until smooth, cover with a kitchen towel, and let the dough sit for 15 minutes.

After 15 minutes, divide the dough into 12 dough balls.

Heat the oil in a medium skillet over medium heat. Press a dough ball between 2 sheets of wax paper and roll it out to a 4-inch diameter circle using a rolling pin. If you are using a tortilla press, cover the bottom plate with plastic wrap, and place a dough ball onto the plastic. Cover the dough with another sheet of plastic, close the press and apply a slight amount of pressure to the lever. (Rolling or pressing these tostada shells is similar to making corn tortillas, but these will be a little thicker, and smaller in diameter.)

Before you fry the tostado shell, pinch off a tiny piece of dough and drop it into the oil. If it sizzles, the oil is ready. Remove the top sheet of wax paper or plastic from the tortilla. Pick the tortilla up with the bottom sheet of wax paper or plastic intact, peeling it off as you carefully place the shell into the hot oil.

Fry each tostado shell in the hot oil for 1 to 2 minutes, turning, until both sides are golden brown and crisp. Use a slotted spoon or spider to remove the tortillas from the oil, and drain on paper towels.

To make the shrimp and guacamole topping, heat the oil in a large skillet over medium heat. Add the shrimp and jalapeño, season with ¼ teaspoon salt, and ⅛ teaspoon black pepper, and sauté for 3 to 4 minutes, stirring frequently, until the shrimp turns pink and opaque. Set aside.

Cut the avocado in half and remove the pit. Use a spoon to scoop out the meat, and place it in a shallow bowl. Using the tines of a fork, mash the avocado, and stir together with the lime juice and the remaining salt and pepper.
Spread a layer of avocado onto each tostada shell, and top each one with a spoonful of the jalapeño shrimp mixture. Serve warm or at room temperature.

Most tostadas are best eaten as soon as they are made. However, you can fry the shells a day or so early and store at room temperature in an airtight container.

SERRANO POR DOS

Many types of jalapeno poppers have made their way onto restaurant menus and appetizer trays for the last couple of decades. Some versions of the cheese-stuffed peppers are deep-fried and others are wrapped in bacon. Serrano por dos is a sleek, sophisticated version with an ever-so-sublte touch of piloncillo sugar to offset the heat of the serrano pepper. ★ *NOTE: Most piloncillo sugar is molded into a cone before packaging (see photo below). You can easily grate the hardened sugar, as needed, with a nutmeg grater or micoplane.*

serves 8

8 serrano chiles
4 ounces cream cheese
2 tablespoons grated piloncillo sugar, or brown sugar
1/3 pound serrano ham, thinly sliced

With gloved hands, rinse the chiles and pat them dry. Slice each one in half lengthwise. Use a spoon or paring knife to remove the seeds and membranes, and discard.

Preheat the oven to 425° F.

Place the chiles cut-side up on a baking sheet. Fill each chile with cream cheese, and sprinkle a pinch or two of grated piloncillo, or brown sugar, over the cream cheese.

Cut the serrano ham slices into 1-inch-wide strips. Wrap each stuffed serrano chile with a strip of serrano ham. Bake for 15 minutes, or until the ham begins to brown and crisp.

Leftovers can be refrigerated in an airtight container for up to 1 week. Reheat them on a baking sheet in a 425° F oven for about 10 minutes.

TIP: If you fear the intensity of heat from a certain variety of chiles or peppers, you can check the level of heat on what is called a Scoville chart, found online and very useful if you are not familiar with a type of chile or pepper.

BLACK BEAN CHICKEN EMPANADAS

Chicken and black beans are a classic empanada filling, and taste even better mixed with corn, peppers and onions. Leftover grilled chicken is a great choice to use in this recipe but any cooked chicken will work, even the rotisserie chicken from the market. ★ *The empanada dough can be made ahead of time and frozen, then thawed when you're ready to use, the same way you might handle pie crust dough. Black Bean Chicken Empanadas taste great whether they're hot out of the oven, or at room temperature.*

serves 6

Filling

2 cups cooked chicken breasts, shredded

I cup cooked black beans (recipe, p. 93), drained, or canned black beans, drained and rinsed

I cup fresh or frozen corn

I fresh jalapeño, stemmed, seeded, and finely diced

½ red bell pepper, stemmed, seeded, and diced

½ Spanish onion, peeled and diced

⅓ cup light sour cream

⅓ cup grated cheddar cheese

2 tablespoons chopped fresh cilantro leaves

I tablespoon fresh lime juice

Salt and pepper, to taste

Dough

2 ½ cups all-purpose flour

½ teaspoon salt

4 ounces cream cheese, room temperature

½ cup (I stick) butter, room temperature

½ cup vegetable shortening, cold

I egg

I tablespoon milk or water

In a large skillet over medium heat, stir together the cooked chicken, beans, corn, jalapeño, bell pepper, and onion until well combined. Stir in the sour cream and cheddar cheese until well blended. Add ¼ cup water and stir to combine. Add the cilantro, lime juice, salt, and pepper, and continue to cook over medium heat, stirring, for 10 minutes, or until the mixture is heated through. Remove from the heat and allow the chicken to cool while you prepare the dough.

In a small mixing bowl, sift together the flour and salt.

With an electric mixer, or a food processor equipped with a stainless steel mixing blade, mix the cream cheese and butter until well blended. Gradually add in the flour and salt mixture. Then add the cold shortening and mix until the dough comes together. Turn the dough out onto a well-floured surface and use your floured hands to form a round disk. Roll the dough out with a lightly floured rolling pin to about a ⅛- to ¹⁄₁₆-inch thickness. I typically cut the dough into 5-inch diameter circles using a small saucer as a template. (If you make smaller circles, you don't have much room for the filling.) Re-roll the remaining dough, being cautious not to overwork it, and pat it out again to cut out more circles.

Preheat the oven to 375° F.

Place the circles of dough on parchment-lined baking sheets. Spoon 2 to 3 tablespoons of the chicken filling onto each circle of dough.

Beat the egg in a small bowl with I tablespoon milk or water. Brush the edges of the dough with the egg mixture to act as a glue to seal the dough. Fold the dough over the filling to form a half-circle and crimp the edges of the dough, using your thumb and forefinger or the tines of a fork to seal. Cut 3 small slits in the top of each empanada to allow steam to escape. Brush the tops with the remaining egg mixture, and bake for 20 to 25 minutes, until the crust is golden brown.

These tasty empanadas will keep, covered and refrigerated, for up to three days. Reheat on a baking sheet in a 350° F oven for about 15 minutes.

OVEN-FRIED TOMATILLOS
WITH ASADERO CHEESE AND OREGANO OIL

Each time my aunt goes back to our hometown for a visit, she likes to stop at the local grocery and pick up a big block of mild, salty Asadero cheese to bring back home. One Indian summer evening, she and my cousin ended up bringing home a load of green tomatoes, too. They did what all good Southerners would do: they sliced them, dipped them in batter, and fried them. ★ My timing was impeccable when I stopped in to visit them that night. As I walked into the kitchen, the aroma of fresh tomatoes and hot sauce permeated the air. Each batch of fried green tomatoes was topped with a slice of the Asadero and a drizzle of hot sauce. ★ This lighter version is baked instead of fried. Because tomatillos are readily available at most markets year-round, the tangy taste makes this a fabulous Southwestern adaptation of a traditional Southern favorite.

serves 6

6 tomatillos, husked, rinsed and
    patted dry
2 tablespoons salt
1 cup milk
2 tablespoons white vinegar
1 egg
½ cup cornmeal
½ cup dry, unseasoned breadcrumbs
1 teaspoon garlic powder
½ teaspoon chili powder
½ pound Asadero, or other mild cheese,
    sliced or cut into small rounds
Oregano oil, or olive oil

Place a wire baking rack on top of a baking sheet. Slice the tomatillos into ½- inch thick slices and place them on the wire rack. Sprinkle them generously with salt on both sides, and let them rest for 10 minutes.

Position the oven rack a little higher than the middle, but not all the way at the top of the oven. Preheat the oven to 450° F.

In a small bowl, pour the milk and vinegar together. Let the mixture rest for 1 minute, then stir. Whisk the egg into the milk mixture until well blended.

In a separate small bowl, mix together the cornmeal, breadcrumbs, garlic powder, and the chili powder.

Pat the tomatillo slices with paper towels to remove any excess salt and moisture. Dip each slice into the milk mixture, and then into the bread-crumb mixture, and place on the wire baking rack. (NOTE: The skin on a tomatillo is waxier than the skin of a tomato, so be aware that the breading will not adhere to the sides of the slices.) Bake for 25 minutes, or until the tomatillos turn a light golden brown.

Layer 1 slice of baked tomatillo with one slice of Asadero, or other mild cheese. Drizzle with oil and your favorite hot sauce and serve with pick-led pepper mix on the side.

For a festive presentation to share, stack multiple layers of tomatillos and cheese, then top with 2 or 3 pieces of Pint of Pickled Peppes (recipe, p. 16) skewered on a toothpick, and a dash of hot sauce to taste.

SOPA

Soups, stews, caldo, and chili as a first course, or a complete meal

SLOW-COOKER CHICKEN ENCHILADA SOUP

The weekends are great for experimenting with slow-cooker recipes, but nothing quite compares to coming home after a busy weekday to the inviting aroma of dinner ready in the crock pot. ★ *This slow-cooker recipe produces tender chicken breasts infused with the aromatic flavors of the Southwest.* ★ *The addition of Queso Fresco (recipe, p. 32) makes this soup rich and creamy, much the way Italian soups use a Parmesan rind to create that extra flavor and creaminess.*

serves 8 to 10

2 boneless, skinless chicken breast halves
1 (28-ounce) can diced tomatoes, with juice
1 (15-ounce) can chili beans, with juice
½ cup diced roasted green chiles (recipe, p. 38)
3 cups chicken broth, or stock
2 cups fresh or frozen corn
1 Spanish onion, peeled and diced
2 cloves garlic, peeled and finely minced
1 fresh jalapeño, stemmed, seeded, and finely diced
2 teaspoons chili powder
1 teaspoon cumin
10 ounces Queso Fresco cheese, finely crumbled (recipe, p. 32)
¼ cup vegetable oil
8 corn tortillas cut into small strips (recipe, p. 28)
Salt to taste
½ cup grated cheese, such as Colby jack, pepper jack, or cheddar

Optional toppings
Juice of 1 lime
Fresh cilantro leaves, chopped
Light sour cream

Place the chicken breasts into a slow-cooker and add the tomatoes with juice, chili beans with juice, the diced green chiles, chicken broth or stock, corn, diced onion, garlic, and jalapeño. Stir to combine. Add the chili powder, cumin, and crumbled queso fresco, and stir to incorporate.

Cook on low for 8 to 9 hours, or on high for 4 to 4 ½ hours. After that time, remove the chicken breasts and let them cool enough to handle. Take this opportunity to vigorously stir the soup to ensure the crumbled cheese is completely melted and blended into the broth.

Heat the oil in a medium skillet over medium heat. Test one tortilla strip to see if it sizzles. When it sizzles, add half of the tortilla strips to the skillet and cook 1 to 2 minutes, turning, until golden brown and crispy on both sides. Drain the tortillas on a paper towel-lined plate. Repeat the process until all the tortillas are fried. While the tortillas are still hot, sprinkle them with a pinch of salt, as desired.

Shred the cooled chicken with two forks, return it to the slow-cooker pot, Salt to taste, and stir to combine.

Serve warm and top individual servings with fried tortilla strips, grated cheese, and other optional toppings of your choice.

Leftover soup may be refrigerated in an airtight container for 1 week, or frozen for up to 3 months. Reheat in the slow-cooker or on the stovetop.

CALDO DE POLLO

Caldo is the Spanish word for a broth-based soup, and Caldo de Pollo is chicken soup. Even in Mexico, chicken soup is thought to be a cure for common ailments. Most families have their own way of preparing this Mexican soup—and it is often very different from household to household, or familia to familia. This one is a combination of chicken and vegetables, with flavorful spices that create a warm, welcoming bowl of comfort. ★ For another serving option, omit the potatoes in this recipe and ladle the soup over a bowl of steamed rice.

serves 6

2 pounds chicken, whole or pieces,
   skin on
1 ½ teaspoons salt
1 teaspoon black pepper
2 ½ teaspoons chili powder
1 teaspoon cumin
1 teaspoon dried oregano
1 Spanish onion, peeled and diced, and
   divided
2 cloves garlic, peeled and finely minced,
   and divided
2 russet potatoes, peeled and diced
4 carrots, peeled and diced
2 single celery stalks with leaves, diced
1 cup fresh or frozen corn
½ head all-seasons green cabbage, cut
   into 1-inch cubes

Optional topping
Diced avocado

Place the chicken in a large stockpot with 2 to 3 quarts water, or enough to cover. Add the salt, pepper, chili powder, cumin, and oregano. Add ½ the diced onion and 1 minced clove garlic. Bring the water to a boil over high heat, then reduce the heat to medium and continue cooking for 30 to 45 minutes. (If you are cooking a whole chicken, the cooking time is 45 minutes; if you have chicken pieces, then cook for 30 minutes.) Test for doneness, by piercing the chicken with a fork.

When the juice runs clear, remove the chicken from the pot and set on a cutting board to cool enough to handle. Skim the top of the broth and reduce the heat to low.

When the chicken has cooled, remove the skin and debone the chicken; discard skins and bones. Use your hands to shred the chicken into bite-size pieces.

Taste the broth before adding the vegetables. If the broth doesn't have enough flavor, stir in a chicken bouillon cube or two. Add the chicken, the remaining onion and garlic, and the vegetables to the broth in the stockpot, and increase the heat to medium-high. Bring the caldo just to a boil, then reduce the heat to medium-low and simmer for 30 minutes.

Pour into bowls, top with diced avocado, if desired, and serve with warm, buttered tortillas.

Caldo can be refrigerated in an airtight container for up to 1 week. Simply reheat in a saucepan or stockpot over medium heat.

ROASTED CHICKEN-CORN CHOWDER

Corn is a predominate ingredient in Southwestern cuisine and for most recipes fresh corn is better, but in the winter months frozen corn can be used to make more chilies, soups, and chowders. In this recipe the ears of corn are roasted, so you will need to thaw the corn and pat it dry before roasting. ★ *The addition of coconut milk to this chowder in place of heavy cream is a perfect, healthy balance to the bold Southwestern flavors.*

serves 6 to 8

1 whole garlic head
1 tablespoon olive oil
Pinch salt and pepper
2 chicken breast halves, skin on
1 teaspoon crushed red pepper flakes
¼ teaspoon salt
½ teaspoon dried oregano
4 ears fresh or frozen corn
½ Spanish onion, peeled
1 red bell pepper, halved, stemmed, and seeded
1 poblano pepper, halved, stemmed, and seeded
2 small russet potatoes, peeled and diced
1 teaspoon ground black pepper, divided
1 teaspoon chili powder
1 tablespoon all-purpose flour, or masa harina, found in most supermarkets
2 ½ cups chicken broth
1 ½ cups unsweetened coconut milk
1 lime, cut into wedges
2 tablespoons fresh cilantro leaves

Preheat the oven to 425° F.

Cut a ½-inch from the tip end of the garlic. Brush the garlic with oil and sprinkle with a pinch of salt and pepper. Wrap it in foil.

Brush the chicken with the remaining olive oil and sprinkle with the red pepper flakes, ¼ teaspoon salt, and the oregano. Place the chicken and foil-wrapped garlic on a roasting pan and bake for 40 to 45 minutes. Test the meat for doneness. The juices will run clear when the chicken is pierced with a fork. Set the pan aside to cool.

Place the ears of corn and the onion on a baking sheet. Place the pepper halves, cut-side down on the baking sheet. Increase the oven temperature to 475° F and roast the vegetables for 20 minutes, turning the corn half-way through the roasting, until the tops of the peppers and the onion are golden brown. NOTE: The corn may take up to an additional 10 minutes for some of the kernels to brown and caramelize.

When the chicken is cool enough to handle, remove the skin and debone. Dice the chicken into bite-size pieces and place in a stockpot.

Squeeze the roasted garlic from its skins onto a cutting board, smash the cloves into small pieces, and add those to the pot. Cut the kernels from the corncobs and add those to the stockpot. Remove the outer skins of the peppers and onion, dice them both and add to the mixture in the stockpot along with the diced potatoes. Sprinkle the pepper, chili powder, and flour (or masa harina) into the pot, and stir to coat the chicken.

Add the chicken broth and coconut milk to the pot, and stir to combine. Cover and cook over medium heat for 20 to 30 minutes, or until the potatoes are tender. Reduce the heat to medium-low if the pot begins to boil.

Top each serving with a squeeze of fresh lime juice, and sprinkle with fresh cilantro leaves.

Leftover chowder may be refrigerated in an airtight container for up to 1 week. Reheat in a saucepan or stockpot over medium heat.

ZUCCHINI SOPA
WITH STUFFED SQUASH BLOSSOMS

If you thought squash blossoms were just for Italian cuisine, think again. The Southwestern Indians have long appreciated these delightful blossoms, and you've probably seen the turquoise squash blossom necklace designs without realizing they were also a staple of the Southwestern diet. ★

serves 6

2 tablespoons butter
2 small zucchini, diced
1 single celery stalk, diced
1 small Spanish onion, peeled and diced
4 medium potatoes, peeled and diced
3 cups chicken broth
2 cups low-fat milk
Salt and pepper to taste
1 ¾ cups grated cheddar cheese

Optional Topping
1 teaspoon chile oil per serving

Stuffed Squash Blossoms
6 fresh squash blossoms, cleaned and trimmed
3 ounces pepper-jack cheese, cut into 6 equal pieces to fit inside the squash blossoms
¾ cup cake flour
¾ cup beer, or soda water
Vegetable oil for frying

Melt the butter in a large pot over medium heat. Add the zucchini, celery, and onion, and sauté for 2 minutes. Add the potatoes and chicken broth, and cook for 20 minutes, or until the potatoes are tender. Remove from the heat and let the mixture cool slightly.

While the potatoes are cooking, prepare the fried squash blossoms, stuffing 1 piece of pepper-jack cheese inside each blossom, and twist the tips of each blossom together to help secure the cheese during cooking.

Heat ¾-inch oil in a small skillet over medium heat.

Whisk together the flour and beer in small bowl to create the batter for the blossoms. Dip each stuffed blossom into the batter to fully coat. Test the heat of the oil with a drop of batter; when it sizzles, begin frying the blossoms. Cook 1 minute on each side, turning, until the blossoms are a light golden brown. Drain the blossoms on paper towels.

To complete the sopa, using a handheld potato masher, mash the zucchini-potato mixture in the pot until smooth, but with some texture remaining. Add the milk, stirring until well blended. Return the pot to medium heat and cook for 4 to 5 minutes to heat through but do not let it come to a boil. Add salt and pepper to taste, remove from the heat, and stir in the grated cheese until just melted.

Ladle the sopa into serving bowls and top each serving with a squash blossom, and a drizzle of chile oil, as desired.

Zucchini Sopa is best served immediately, but may be refrigerated in an airtight container for up to 1 week. To reheat, slowly warm over medium-low heat to ensure the cheese does not separate. Leftover squash blossoms may be refrigerated, covered, for a few days. Reheat on a baking sheet in a 350° F oven for 15 minutes.

TEXAS BEEF & BEAN CHILI

Chili is a household staple in the Southwest, and it comes in many forms. Some folks are purists and would never add beans to a pot of chili. But for me, the combination of textures and the nutritional value can't be beat. ★ This particular recipe is a Texas-style chili.

serves 10

3 pounds lean ground sirloin

2 tablespoons olive oil

1 large Spanish onion, peeled and diced

3 cloves garlic, minced

6 tablespoons chili powder

2 teaspoons salt

1 ½ teaspoons cumin

1 ½ teaspoons dried oregano

1 teaspoon black pepper

6 tablespoons all-purpose flour, or masa
   harina, found in most supermarkets

5 cups beef stock

4 cups tomato juice

2 cups dried Pinto or Anasazi beans,
   sorted and rinsed

2 tablespoons chipotle-adobo paste, or
   canned chipotles in adobo sauce,
   finely minced

Whole fresh jalapeños, optional

Saltine crackers

Optional toppings

Corn chips, your choice brand

Longhorn, or other cheese, grated

Raw onion, diced

Pickled jalapeños, sliced

Preheat the oven to 350° F.

Brown the ground sirloin in olive oil in a large Dutch oven over medium heat. Add the onion, garlic, chili powder, salt, cumin, oregano, and black pepper and stir until blended. Sprinkle with the flour, or masa harina, and stir until well combined. Stir in the beef stock, tomato juice, dried beans, and chipotle-adobo paste, increase the heat to medium-high, and bring to a boil. When the chili begins to boil, cover and place in the preheated oven. Cook for 1 ½ hours.

At the end of the cooking time, transfer the Dutch oven to your stovetop over low heat. Remove the lid to allow the chili to thicken. (Add the whole jalapeños, if desired.) Simmer for 1 hour, stirring occasionally, until the beans are tender.

Serve with corn muffins or saltine crackers.

I like to make a batch of this chili and freeze it. It will keep, frozen, for up to 3 months in an airtight container; or leftovers can be refrigerated for up to 1 week. The flavors intensify the longer it is refrigerated, so be aware that the jalapeños you put in will add even more heat to your leftovers. The chili can be slowly reheated in a crock pot for 2 to 3 hours, or reheat in a heavy-bottom pan on the stovetop over medium heat.

Chili versus Chile

People in the Southwest are crazy about their chile ... and their chili. When I eat a bowl of chili with beef and beans, or purchase a container of chili powder, it is spelled with an "i" on the end. But when talking about certain varieties of peppers, the word ends with an "e." Anything made with chile peppers or freshly ground dried chile pods is referred to as "chile" in the Southwest.

Remove the seeds and membranes to reduce the heat level of most any variety of pepper. Wear gloves when cutting and seeding chiles—and definitely do not rub your eyes. I can handle varieties of green chiles and jalapeños, but serranos call for the gloves. Or, if I am handling a large quantity of any type of pepper, I also wear gloves for the task.

Here's a helpful tip: When roasting or charring fresh chiles (as on page 38), the skin will blister and toughen, and should be peeled off and discarded. However, the skins will soften during other cooking methods and may then be left intact. Additionally, when using dried red chiles (as on page 37), I typically strain the mixture and discard the dried skins.

SLOW-COOKER CARNITAS STEW

Carnitas means "little meats." Traditionally, it is made with chunks of heavily marbled pork and slowly braised in lard for up to 4 hours, similar to confit—very tasty, but not so heart-healthy. In this nutritious version the pork is seared in a small amount of olive oil, then braised in a flavorful green chile broth to create one of the most popular stews of the Southwest. ★ Nothing could be better than to serve this with a stack of warm flour tortillas.

serves 6

1 tablespoon olive oil
1 (2- to 3-pound) pork roast
2 cups diced roasted green chiles (recipe, p. 38)
2 bottles beer (your choice brand), or 3 cups vegetable broth
1 teaspoon salt, divided
1 teaspoon coarsely ground black pepper, divided
1 teaspoon chili powder
1 teaspoon onion powder
½ teaspoon cumin
½ teaspoon smoked paprika
2 pounds potatoes, peeled and diced

Optional Topping
¾ cup light sour cream
1 fresh jalapeño, stemmed, seeded, and diced
Juice of 1 lime
Pinch of salt

Heat the oil in a large skillet over medium-high heat.

Season the roast with ½ teaspoon salt and ½ teaspoon ground black pepper. Sear the roast in the hot oil for 1 to 2 minutes on each side, until the meat is a deep golden brown color.

Place the green chiles and beer (or broth) into a large slow-cooker. Stir in the remaining salt and pepper, along with the chili powder, onion powder, cumin, and smoked paprika, then add the roast. Cook on high for 4 hours.

Add the potatoes and 1 cup of water and cook an additional 4 hours on high. Remove the roast and place on a cutting board. Use two forks to shred the meat, then stir the shredded meat back into the stew and serve hot.

To make the optional topping, stir together all ingredients and keep chilled. Serve a dollop atop each bowl of stew, if desired.

I like to make this over the weekend and save it for a weekday treat. Refrigerate in an airtight container for up to 1 week. Reheat in a saucepan or stockpot over medium heat until warmed through.

TEX-MEX POSOLE CASSOULET

Posole is a very popular dish in the Southwest. It is a thick Mexican soup made with hominy and pork. The cassoulet originated in the southwestern region of France and is a bean stew, or casserole, often containing pork. We really put the pig to work in this dish with the addition of cubed pork chops and bacon. ★ *This recipe may sound like a contradiction of terms. Julia Child would probably scold me, who knows. She had a very open mind about food, though, and I'll bet she would love this dish.*

serves 6 to 8

1 cup dried pinto or Anasazi beans,
    sorted and rinsed
4 boneless center-cut pork chops,
    cubed
1/3 cup all-purpose flour
2 tablespoons olive oil
8 slices thick-cut bacon, cut into
    small pieces
1 Spanish onion, peeled and diced
1 teaspoon salt
4 cloves garlic, minced
2 tablespoons fresh cilantro leaves,
chopped, and divided
1/4 cup tomato paste
2 tablespoons chipotle-adobo paste, or
    canned chipotles in adobe sauce,
    finely minced
6 cups chicken broth
1 cup dry white wine
1 (15-ounce) can hominy
1 cup cornbread croutons

Place the beans in a pot with enough water to cover and soak overnight. (If you don't have time to pre-soak, bring the water to a boil over high heat, cover the pot of beans with a lid, reduce the heat to medium, and simmer for a few minutes. Remove the beans from the heat and let them stand for 1 hour while your prepare the remaining ingredients). Drain the water from the beans.

Toss the pork chop cubes in the flour to coat.

Heat the oil in a Dutch oven over medium-high heat. Working in batches so you don't overcrowd the pot, sear the pork for 1 minute on each side, turning so the meat browns evenly. Add the bacon pieces and continue cooking until the bacon begins to brown. Stir in the onion and salt. Add the beans, garlic, 1 tablespoon cilantro leaves, tomato paste, chipotle-adobo paste, and chicken broth. Bring to a boil, then cover and reduce the heat to medium-low, and simmer for 1 hour.

Preheat the oven to 350° F.

Stir in the wine and hominy, then cover and place the Dutch oven in the oven for 1 hour and 15 minutes.

Top individual servings with the remaining cilantro, and sprinkle with the cornbread croutons. Serve hot.

Leftover cassoulet may be refrigerated in an airtight container for up to 1 week. Reheat leftovers in a saucepan over medium heat.

TIP: Tubes of tomato paste are a great product to keep on hand to use when you do not need an entire can. Also, fresh cornbread croutons can be easily made with bits of leftover cornbread cut into cubes and toasted in a skillet with a little butter over medium heat until golden.

NACHO MAMA'S BEANS & RICE

Southwestern sides so good you'll beg for seconds

HOMINY AU GRATIN

If processing corn into hominy is not your idea of spending an afternoon or evening, no worries, there are several good options. Canned hominy is commonly used in many Southwestern dishes, and there are also good frozen brands; my favorite is Bueno hominy. ★ *Flavor combinations for hominy casseroles are often similar to casseroles made with grits. Pair this dish with a good steak for an alternative to fries or a baked potato. This is my home-cooked version of a fabulous casserole I tasted at a steakhouse in Buffalo Gap, Texas.*

serves 4 to 6

2 (15-ounce) cans yellow hominy,
  drained and rinsed

½ cup diced roasted green chiles (recipe,
  p. 38)

2 cloves garlic, peeled and minced

½ teaspoon black pepper

¼ teaspoon salt

I teaspoon unsalted butter, for buttering
  the dish

I cup heavy cream

I cup milk

4 ounces (½ cup) grated Longhorn, or
  cheddar cheese

In a medium mixing bowl, add the hominy, green chiles, garlic, black pepper, and salt, and stir to combine.

Preheat the oven to 350° F. Butter an 8 x 8-inch baking dish, or 4 to 6 individual ramekins.

Pour the hominy mixture into the baking dish, or ramekins, and then pour the heavy cream and the milk over the hominy. Bake uncovered for 30 minutes. Remove the casserole from the oven, top with grated cheese, and continue baking another 8 to 10 minutes, until the mixture is bubbly and the cheese has melted. Serve warm.

Leftovers may be refrigerated in a tightly covered container for up to I week. Reheat, covered, in a 350° F oven until bubbly.

ANASAZI BEANS

Anasazi beans were originally cultivated by the Anasazi Indians on the dry land of southwestern Colorado. The ones I buy are packaged by the Adobe Milling Company in Dove Creek, Colorado. Dove Creek is also the pinto bean capital of the world; the climate and altitude produce some of the best beans you can buy. ★ *Anasazi beans are a beautiful dark maroon color with bright, white marbling. They are a bit smaller than pinto beans and a little sweeter. Frijoles Rancheros, or "ranch style beans" is a popular preparation for pinto beans in the Southwest. I use Anasazi beans and add lots of fresh flavors.* ★ *Serve with Navajo Tacos, (recipe, p. 128) or Layered Enchiladas, (recipe, p. 112). Although they are a traditional side dish for any Southwestern meal, these beans become the main dish when paired with steamed rice, or mashed as a filling for burritos.*

serves 8 to 10

1 pound dried Anasazi, or pinto beans
6 slices bacon, chopped (or substitute
    chunks of ham, or rinsed salt pork)
2 cloves garlic, peeled and finely minced
1 Spanish onion, peeled and diced
1 fresh or pickled jalapeño, stemmed,
    seeded, and diced
2 Roma tomatoes, diced
2 tablespoons chili powder
1 teaspoon cumin
1 teaspoon salt
1 teaspoon black pepper
½ teaspoon dried oregano

Sort and rinse the dried beans. Place them in a large stockpot with 6 cups water, or enough to cover. Bring the beans to a boil over medium-high heat, then reduce the heat to medium and continue cooking, adding more water as needed.

When the beans begin to soften, add all the remaining ingredients. Reduce the heat to medium-low and continue to cook, stirring occasionally, until the beans are tender. The total cooking time will be 2 ½ to 3 hours.

Leftover beans may be refrigerated in an airtight container for up to 1 week. Reheat the beans in a saucepan over medium heat.

SPANISH RICE

My aunt and uncle from New Mexico may not realize how much of an inspiration they have been for me when it comes to cooking Southwestern cuisine. They taught us the basics. My aunt showed my family how to make the best Spanish rice which goes perfectly with the delicious Stacked Enchiladas (recipe, p. 108) my uncle taught us to make. ★ This side dish is a staple in our household and I am happy to be able to share it with you.

serves 8 to 10

2 tablespoons olive oil

2 cups uncooked long grain white rice

½ cup diced roasted green chiles (recipe, p. 38)

1 small Spanish onion, peeled and finely diced

4 cups chicken broth, or water

3 tablespoon tomato paste

½ teaspoon salt

½ teaspoon black pepper

½ teaspoon garlic powder

¼ teaspoon cumin

In a large skillet over medium heat, add the olive oil and sauté the rice, green chiles, and onion for 5 minutes, stirring often, until the rice turns light brown.

Stir in the broth or water, turn the heat to medium-high, and bring the rice to a boil. Reduce the heat to medium-low and add the tomato paste, salt, black pepper, garlic powder, and cumin, and stir to combine. Cover the skillet and simmer for approximately 20 minutes, or until the rice is tender and the liquid is absorbed.

Leftover rice may be refrigerated in an airtight container for up to a week. Reheat the rice in a saucepan over medium heat, with 1 to 2 tablespoons water to ensure the rice stays moist.

FRESH FIESTA SALAD

Fiesta salad can be made with a wide array of beautiful seasonal vegetables—the fresher, the better. ★ *In the summertime, this is the family choice for a fresh, quick dish to accompany almost any meal.*

serves 6

3 ears corn, shucked and rinsed

3 tablespoons olive oil

1 medium (or 2 small) zucchinis, cut in
 ½-inch cubes

4 green onions, thinly sliced

1 red bell pepper, stemmed, seeded, and
 diced

1 fresh jalapeño, stemmed, seeded and
 finely diced

1 ½ cups grape tomatoes, halved

2 tablespoons fresh cilantro leaves

½ cup crumbled Queso Fresco cheese
 (recipe, p. 32)

Salt and pepper, to taste

Place the corn in a large pot with enough water to cover. Bring to a boil over medium heat, and boil for 2 minutes, then use tongs to remove the corn from the pot and set aside to cool. Once the corn has cooled enough to handle, stand the cobs on end and use a sharp knife to remove the kernels, cutting in a downward motion.

Heat the oil in a large skillet over medium heat. Add the corn, zucchini, onions, bell pepper, and jalapeño and sauté 4 to 5 minutes, until tender. Transfer to a serving bowl and toss with the tomato halves, cilantro, the Queso Fresco, salt, and pepper.

Serve the salad at room temperature, or chilled. Leftover salad may be refrigerated in an airtight container for up to 2 days.

CHILI-LIME CUCUMBERS
WITH JICAMA

A popular refreshment sold by vendors at outdoor markets around the Southwest is a cup of fresh fruits and veggies doused with lime and chiles. There couldn't be anything juicier and more refreshing under a hot sun. Cucumbers and jicama are mixed with a touch of sweet orange that brightens up this fresh, crunchy salad. ★ Serve it with Mesquite Smoked Brisket (recipe, p. 96) or Gulf Coast Street Tacos (recipe, p. 126).

serves 6 to 8

2 cucumbers, peeled, large dice
1 jicama, peeled, large dice
1 orange, peeled and separated into
    sections
Juice of 1 lime, or about 3 tablespoons
½ teaspoon chili powder
Salt to taste

Optional topping
½ cup Mexican Crema with Lime (recipe,
    p. 23)

Place the cucumbers, jicama, and orange sections in a medium mixing bowl. Toss them with the lime juice. Season with the chili powder and salt to taste, and mix well.

As an optional topping, drizzle 1 tablespoon Mexican Crema with Lime over each serving.

Cover with plastic wrap and refrigerate for at least 20 minutes, or until you are ready to serve. Serve cold.

Leftover salad may be refrigerated in an airtight container for 2 to 3 days.

NOTE: A chili-lime flavored salt made by Tajin may be used in place of chili powder and salt. The texture is more coarse than regular chili powder and the flavor is more concentrated, so you may want to use less than this recipe suggests.

CALABACITAS

Squash is a beloved summer staple and it is very evident in many Mexican and Southwestern dishes. Thank goodness we can purchase it year-round in the markets. ★ "Calabacitas" is Spanish for "little squash." It is an assortment of tender, small squashes. The ones used for this dish are best when the skin is still thin and seeds are tiny and tender. Their mild flavor combines perfectly with sweet corn and onion. ★ This dish is the epitome of summertime on a plate when served alongside grilled steaks, or chicken.

serves 6

2 ears fresh corn
1 teaspoon olive oil
1 teaspoon butter
1 sweet onion, such as Texas 1015 or
   Vidalia, peeled and diced
3 cloves garlic, peeled and minced
2 pounds squash — any or mixed
   varieties, cut into bite-size pieces
1/8 teaspoon cayenne
Salt and pepper to taste

Optional Toppings
2 tablespoons fresh herbs of your choice,
   chopped
1/4 cup crumbled Queso Fresco, (recipe,
   p. 32)

Remove the husks and silks from the corn, and rinse the cobs. Stand the cobs on end and remove the kernels, cutting in a downward motion with a sharp knife. Set the kernels aside.

Heat the oil and butter in a large skillet over medium heat. Sauté the onion for 3 minutes, until tender. Add the garlic and cook for 1 minute, then stir in the squash, corn, and cayenne. Continue cooking for 8 to 10 minutes, stirring occasionally. Season with salt and pepper to taste.

Serve warm with desired toppings.

Leftovers may be refrigerated in an airtight container for up to 1 week. Reheat in a skillet over medium heat for 4 to 5 minutes.

MEXICAN STREET CORN

Mexican Street Corn is a popular snack sold at fairgrounds and festivals all over the Southwest. This version is the perfect side dish for your next backyard barbecue, or with lunch or dinner. ★ *When I was a Girl Scout our troop learned how to make our own drinking cups from a square sheet of paper. The illustration below demonstrates how this simple corn container is made, and it's a fun project to have the kids make at your next cookout.*

serves 4

1 tablespoon olive oil
4 ears fresh corn, shucked and rinsed
1/3 cup light mayonnaise
3 tablespoons unsalted butter, softened
1/4 cup finely grated Parmesan cheese
1/2 teaspoon chili powder
1/8 teaspoon salt
1/8 teaspoon black pepper
1 lime, quartered
2 tablespoons chopped fresh cilantro
    leaves

Prepare an outdoor grill, or heat a grill pan over medium heat.

Place 1 tablespoon olive oil in a small dish and brush each ear of corn with the oil. Place the corn directly onto the hot grill or grill pan and cook for 2 to 3 minutes on each side to char the kernels. Remove the corn with tongs, and set aside to cool.

When the corn has cooled enough to handle, stand the cobs on end and, using a sharp knife, cut in a downward motion to remove the kernels.

In a medium mixing bowl, stir together the mayonnaise, butter, and Parmesan cheese until well blended. Add the chili powder, salt, and black pepper, and stir to combine. Fold the corn kernels into the mayonnaise mixture until the kernels are well coated.

Serve chilled, or at room temperature, with a squeeze of fresh lime, and a sprinkling of fresh cilantro on each serving.

Leftovers may be refrigerated in an airtight container for up to 1 week. Stir again before serving.

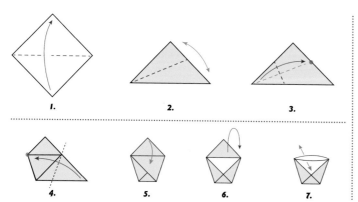

Paper Corn Pockets

1. Start with an 8-inch square sheet of paper; fold in half to create a triangle
2. Fold top corner down to baseline and unfold to create a crease
3. Fold left corner up to the crease line
4. Fold right corner to opposite side
5. Fold front flap toward the front
6. Fold back flap over the back
7. Open finished drinking cup

BAKED ARROZ
WITH GREEN CHILE AND ROASTED GARLIC

Baked arroz, or baked rice, is similar to rice pilaf, and this version is loaded with savory Southwestern flavors; the roasted garlic and green chile will compliment main dishes like Filet Mignon with Chipotle Pan Sauce (recipe p. 106) or Chicken Tinga Tacos (recipe p. 135). ★ *The result is a fluffy, tender rice that will pair beautifully with many of your favorite main dishes.*

serves 4 to 6

1 head garlic
1 tablespoon, plus 1 teaspoon olive oil
1 teaspoon salt, divided
½ teaspoon black pepper, divided
1 ½ cups long grain rice
3 cups chicken stock, or broth
½ cup diced roasted green chiles (recipe, p. 38)
1 tablespoon butter

Preheat the oven to 400° F.

Cut ½-inch off of the tip end of the garlic and brush with 1 teaspoon oil, then sprinkle with ½ teaspoon salt and ¼ teaspoon pepper. Wrap the head of garlic in foil and roast for 10 minutes in the preheated oven.

While the garlic is roasting, place the rice in a Dutch oven, or other oven-proof pot with a lid. Stir in the remaining tablespoon of oil to thoroughly coat the rice. Brown the rice over medium heat for 5 minutes, stirring often. Add the chicken stock or broth to the rice, increase the heat to medium high, and bring to a boil. Reduce the oven temperature to 350° F, cover the rice and bake for 25 minutes alongside the garlic.

Remove the garlic and rice from the oven, leaving the oven turned on. Squeeze the roasted garlic out onto a cutting board and roughly chop. Stir the garlic, green chiles, butter, and the remaining salt and pepper into the rice. Cover, and continue baking for 10 minutes.

Before serving, use a fork to fluff the rice and serve warm.

Leftover rice can be refrigerated in an airtight container for up to 1 week. Reheat the rice in a saucepan over medium heat, along with 1 to 2 tablespoons water, if additional moisture is needed.

COWBOY SWEET POTATO CASSEROLE

Chipotle pepper provides a little heat and smokiness to this dish, balancing well with the sweetness of the piloncillo sugar. The bacon and sour cream also add savory notes to a dish that is traditionally very sweet. ★

serves 8

5 large (approximately 5 pounds) sweet potatoes
1 pound sliced bacon, cooked crispy, then drained, and crumbled
1 chipotle pepper (canned, in adobo sauce), finely diced
½ cup light sour cream
¼ cup unsalted butter, softened, plus more for baking dish
¼ cup grated piloncillo sugar, or brown sugar
⅛ teaspoon salt
⅛ teaspoon cinnamon

Preheat the oven to 425° F.

Scrub the sweet potatoes and pat them dry. Using the tines of a fork, pierce each sweet potato several times, place them on a baking sheet, and roast for 50 to 60 minutes, or until they are fork tender. Set them aside to cool slightly.

Prepare the bacon crumbles and set aside.

Reduce the oven heat to 400° F.

Peel the sweet potatoes, transfer to a large mixing bowl, and mash them with a handheld potato masher. Add the chopped chipotle pepper, the crumbled bacon (reserving ¼ cup for the topping), sour cream, butter, sugar, salt, and cinnamon, and stir together until well combined.

Butter a 2-quart baking dish. Add the sweet potato mixture and top with the remaining crumbled bacon. Bake for 40 minutes. Serve warm.

Leftovers may be refrigerated in an airtight container for up to 1 week. To reheat, transfer to a baking dish, cover with foil, and cook in a 400° F oven for 20 minutes, or until heated through.

THREE MELON MANGO SALAD

Fresh melons and mango taste great all on their own, but add this tangy, kicked up dressing to make this salad the star of your meal. It's ideal for a light lunch or a healthy snack. ★ *This salad is a staple at Southwestern fairs and markets, and is a popular Mexican street food.*

serves 6 to 8

1 ½ cups watermelon, large dice
1 cup cantaloupe, large dice
1 cup honeydew melon, large dice
2 mangos, peeled and diced (see how-to, p. 34)

Dressing
Juice of 2 or 3 limes, or about ¹/₃ cup
Zest of 1 lime
1 tablespoon honey
¼ teaspoon chili powder
¹/₈ teaspoon salt

In a large serving dish, toss together the watermelon, cantaloupe, honeydew melon, and mango.

In a separate small bowl, whisk together the lime juice, lime zest, honey, chili powder, and salt.

Add the dressing to the fruit and gently fold to evenly coat the fruit.

Refrigerate the salad for at least 20 minutes to serve chilled, or you may serve at room temperature.

Leftovers may be refrigerated in an airtight container for 2 or 3 days. If you are making this salad a day or two before your dinner, refrigerate the dressing and fruit separately, and dress the salad just before serving.

FRESH YELLOW SQUASH SALAD

The yogurt dressing in this cool, refreshing salad recipe creates a creamy, nutrient-packed dressing. ★ *Serve this salad as lunch, or with Carne Asada (recipe, p. 100) for dinner.*

serves 4

2 medium (or 3 small) yellow squash
¼ medium red onion, finely diced
1 teaspoon fresh basil leaves, finely chopped
1 teaspoon fresh dill, stemmed and roughly chopped
1 teaspoon fresh flat leaf Italian parsley leaves, roughly chopped
½ cup non-fat Greek yogurt, your choice brand
Salt and pepper, to taste

Cut the squash in half lengthwise, leaving the skins on. Slice each half into thin half-circles and transfer them to a medium mixing bowl. Add the onion, basil, dill, and parsley and toss to combine. Add the yogurt and stir to coat. Season with salt and pepper to taste.

Refrigerate this salad for at least 20 minutes before serving. Serve cold.

Leftovers may be refrigerated for up to 2 days in an airtight container. Stir the salad before serving.

SLOW-COOKER BLACK BEANS

Black beans go especially well with Southwestern food, and this slow-cooker recipe is the perfect no-hassle way to get tender, tasty beans. They are high in fiber and protein and are a good source of iron. ★ *Black beans are featured in Black Bean-Chicken Empanadas (recipe, p. 58), and in Gulf of Mexico Sushi Rolls (recipe, p. 52). Make a batch to serve for dinner and store some in the freezer to use when you need them.*

serves 12

1 pound dry black beans
1 Spanish onion, peeled and quartered
2 cloves garlic, peeled and smashed
½ teaspoon salt
¼ teaspoon black pepper
¼ teaspoon cumin

Sort and rinse the dried beans.

Place them in a slow-cooker along with the onion, garlic, salt, pepper, and cumin. Stir in 6 cups water and cover with the lid. Cook on high heat for 4 hours. Taste for tenderness, and to see if additional seasoning is desired. If the beans are not tender enough, continue to cook on high for 1 to 2 hours more, testing for tenderness after 1 hour.

When the beans are done, discard the onion and garlic. Drain off part of the juice, saving some. (Dry beans do not absorb as much liquid in a slow cooker as they do when prepared on the stovetop.) Serve warm.

Leftover beans may be refrigerated in an airtight container for up to 1 week, or frozen (or make an extra batch to freeze) in zip-top freezer bags or other freezer-safe containers for up to 3 months. Thaw the beans before reheating. Reheat in a saucepan over medium heat for 5 to 10 minutes; add 2 to 3 tablespoons of water, if needed.

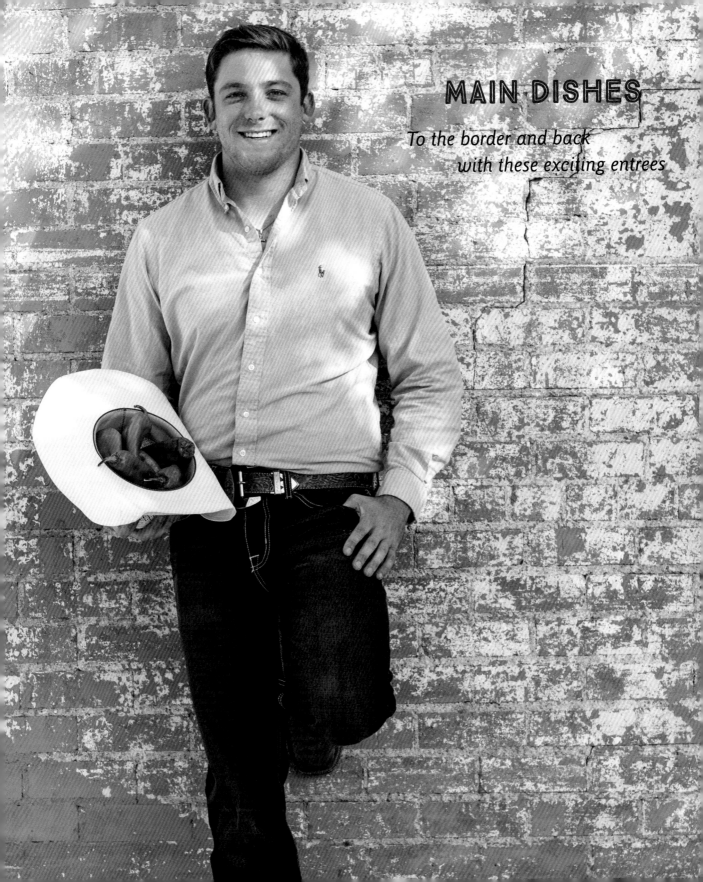

MAIN DISHES

*To the border and back
with these exciting entrees*

MESQUITE SMOKED BRISKET
CHINA BOX-STYLE

PaPaw Dub was a legend in our community when it came to making a juicy, flavorful brisket that always had the perfect smoke-ring around the edges of the meat. He used a giant smoker fabricated out of an old butane tank and it did the job very well. ★ *Serve this brisket with Anasazi Beans (recipe, p. 80), and Pint of Pickled Peppers (recipe, p. 16).* ★ *An untrimmed brisket—the most common way briskets are sold by a butcher or grocer—will have a fat cap on one side of it that will protect the meat from drying out during cooking, and add lots of flavor. It is trimmed away after the meat is smoked.* ★ *To smoke this brisket, we use a La Caja China Box (see page 98) that's made for roasting whole pigs. If you haven't seen one before, the heat source is on top of the meat. To smoke the brisket, we soak wood chips and put them in a small tray, or a smoke box, and place it inside the China Box. This doesn't produce quite the beautiful smoke ring PaPaw's brisket had; however, I guarantee a rich, smoky flavor can be achieved in just a few short hours, versus the 12 or more hours needed for the traditional method. And don't be thrown off by the darkness of the exterior of the meat, the seasoning (dry rub) and the cooking process give it that color, partly from the brown sugar in the dry rub mix. This adds a crispy edge to the irresistible meat you'll find when you slice into it.* ★ *The China Box can accommodate up to 4 briskets at a time if you are cooking for a large event, or want to freeze some for later. Other smokers made specifically for smoking, or standard grills with alternative instructions for smoking may be used.*

serves 6 to 8

Dry Rub

2 tablespoons brown sugar

2 tablespoons salt

2 tablespoons coarsely ground
　black pepper

1 tablespoon garlic powder

1 tablespoon onion powder

1 tablespoon chili powder

1 tablespoon smoked paprika

1 teaspoon cumin

1 teaspoon oregano

1 (12 to 14-pound) untrimmed
　beef brisket

Smoky Chipotle Barbecue Sauce
　(recipe, p. 42)

For this recipe, you will also need to have 3 cups mesquite wood chips, 25 pounds charcoal, 25 pounds lump charcoal, heavy-duty aluminum foil, and 2 large disposable aluminum roasting pans.

Mix the dry rub ingredients together in a small mixing bowl. Rinse the brisket in cool water and pat it dry with paper towels. Apply the dry rub to the brisket overall, and place it, uncovered, in the disposable aluminum pan. Refrigerate, or place the brisket in a cooler packed with ice, for a minimum of 8 hours, or overnight.

Remove the brisket from the refrigerator or cooler 2 hours before cooking.

In a small mixing bowl, soak the wood chips in water for 2 hours. Drain the water and place the chips in an aluminum pie pan, or a smoker box.

China Box Instructions: Place the unwrapped brisket, fat side up, onto the meat rack inside the China Box. Place a disposable aluminum pan underneath the rack to catch the drippings. Place the soaked wood chips in the pie pan, or smoker box, alongside the brisket. Cover the China Box with the ash pan, which acts as a lid. Next, add the charcoal grid.

Add 10 pounds of charcoal and 10 pounds of lump coal (charred wooden brickets) on top of the grid and ignite. In about 20 minutes the coals will be ready to spread. Once you have spread the coals evenly across the grid, start timing the cooking process. *(Continued on the next page)*

MESQUITE SMOKED BRISKET
(continued)

In 1 hour, using heavy gloves or oven mitts, open the box and use tongs to flip the brisket over. Insert a wired thermometer probe into the thickest part of the brisket (an instant read thermometer may be used but it is best to have a wired one you can read from outside the box, as opening the box numerous times will affect the heat inside, affecting the cooking time).

Close the box. Add 5 pounds charcoal and 5 pounds lump coal to the hot coals. Ignite again if necessary. Continue adding coal in this amount every hour. I recommend that you do not open the box again during the remainder of the cooking process. Once the brisket reaches an internal temperature of 190° F, remove it from the China Box. Cooking time will be about 4 hours.

Wrap the brisket in foil and let it rest at room temperature for approximately 1 hour. The internal temperature will continue to rise for a bit, but it is ready to serve when it drops to 190° F (per PaPaw's instructions). PaPaw also liked to let it rest in an empty cooler to help the meat hold its moisture.

Unwrap the brisket, cut off the fat cap and discard it. Slice the brisket on a cutting board that has an indention around the border to collect the juices. You will want to catch this juice to pour over the sliced brisket. Brisket needs to be sliced on the diagonal, against the grain. Using an electric knife makes quick work of slicing this large cut of meat, but a good, sharp carving knife works well, too.

Serve warm or at room temperature with Smoky Chipotle Barbecue Sauce on the side.

Brisket can be tightly wrapped in foil and frozen for up to 3 months, or refrigerated for up to 1 week. When you are ready to reheat, place slices of thawed meat in a baking dish and pour a cup of cola over the beef to keep it moist. Cover the baking dish with foil and place in a preheated 350° F oven for about 20 minutes, until the meat is heated through.

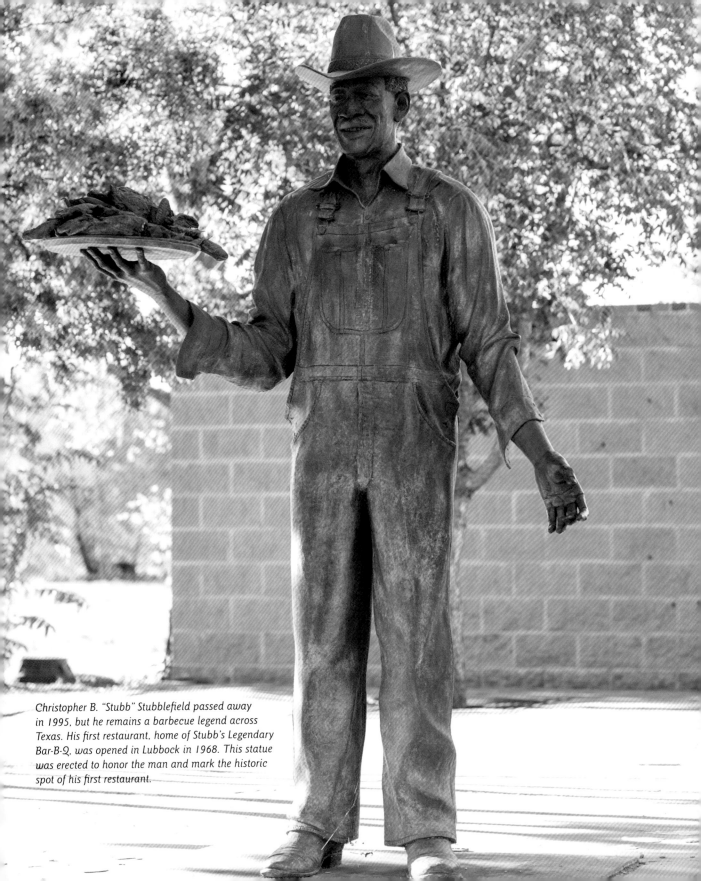

Christopher B. "Stubb" Stubblefield passed away in 1995, but he remains a barbecue legend across Texas. His first restaurant, home of Stubb's Legendary Bar-B-Q, was opened in Lubbock in 1968. This statue was erected to honor the man and mark the historic spot of his first restaurant.

CARNE ASADA

Carne asada means grilled beef. It is prepared in the way you would make a good, marinated steak. It can be served as a taco filling with Handmade Corn or Flour tortillas (recipes, pp. 28, 30), or served alone with a nutritious, healthy side dish, such the Fresh Fiesta Salad (recipe, p. 82). ★ *I was fortunate to be taught how to make carne asada by a dear friend's father who's originally from Mexico. He cooked it over a campfire and served it in a toasty tortilla with refried Pinto beans—perfection!*

serves 4

2 pounds beef skirt steak, silver skin
   removed and discarded
¹/₃ cup freshly squeezed lime juice
2 tablespoons olive oil
¼ teaspoon coarse salt
¼ teaspoon black pepper
3 cloves garlic, peeled and smashed
2 sprigs fresh Mexican oregano, or
   other oregano

To remove the beef skirt silver skin, slip your fingertips under the loose edge of the skin and pull back until you meet resistance. Slip the point of a small sharp knife under the remaining skin and run the knife blade between the skirt steak and the silver skin, pulling the silver skin back with your other hand as you go. Continue down the length of the steak, sliding the knife under the skin while you pull it loose with your other hand.

In a small bowl, whisk together the lime juice, olive oil, salt, pepper, garlic, and oregano. Place the steak in a gallon-size zip-top bag and pour the marinade over the meat. Press the air out of the bag and seal it. Use your hands to rub the marinade completely over the meat, and refrigerate 8 to 10 hours, or overnight.

Prepare an outdoor grill, or preheat a cast-iron grill pan over medium-high heat for 5 minutes.

Remove the meat from the marinade and pat slightly dry with a paper towel.

Place the skirt steak on a grill about 6 inches above the heat, and cook 4 minutes per side. Or, using a grill pan over medium high heat, sear each side, about 30 seconds per side, reduce the heat to medium, and continue to cook 4 minutes on each side. Optimum flavor and texture is achieved when the meat is a bit pink in the center.

Transfer the steak to a cutting board and let it rest 10 to 15 minutes before slicing. (This is a very important step that lets the juices settle.) Slice the meat about ¼-inch thick, on the diagonal across the grain of the meat.

Serve warm, or at room temperature with a nutritious side dish, or build tacos (see photo at right) and top with lightly sauteed strips of bell pepper and onion. Consider adding crunch with ribbons of fresh cabbage or iceberg lettuce, topped off with Charred Salsa (recipe, p. 41).

Extra skirt steak can be wrapped in foil and refrigerated for up to 1 week. Reheat leftovers in their sealed foil packet in a preheated 350° F oven for about 10 minutes.

PESCADO TACOS
WITH RADISH, JICAMA, AND AVOCADO CREMA

Pescado or fish tacos are light and flavorful. The grilled fish is placed in a fresh corn tortilla, topped with the crispy crunch of radishes and jicama, then drizzled with a smooth Avocado Crema. ★ *For extra crunch and texture, add a handful of your favorite greens, such as iceberg lettuce, kale, or arugula.*

serves 4

Avocado Crema
½ cup Mexican Crema with Lime (recipe, p. 23)
½ Haas avocado, skin removed, and diced

4 Tilapia filets
2 teaspoons Swamp Dust, or other Cajun seasoning
6 tablespoons vegetable oil, divided
8 Handmade Corn Tortillas, (recipe, p. 28)
4 radishes, trimmed and thinly sliced
I small jicama, peeled and thinly sliced into I-inch strips

Prepare your outdoor grill, or preheat a cast iron grill pan over medium-high heat for 5 minutes.

Place the Mexican Crema with Lime and the diced avocado into a blender, and blend on medium speed for 30 to 60 seconds, until smooth and creamy. Refrigerate until ready to serve.

Season both sides of the fish filets with Cajun seasoning. With a basting mop or paper towel held with tongs, grease the grill grate or grill pan with 2 tablespoons oil. Place the filets on the grill, or onto a preheated grill pan, reduce the heat to medium, and cook 4 minutes per side. The filets are done when they flake easily with a fork.

Flake the filets into large chunks and set aside.

Heat 4 tablespoons oil in a small skillet over medium heat. Test the temperature of the oil by dropping a small piece of tortilla into the pan; when it sizzles, it is ready. One at a time, place each tortilla into the hot oil and cook for a about 30 seconds on each side, until they are light golden brown and crisp, but still flexible enough to fold. Drain on a paper towel-lined plate.

Build the tacos with flakes of fish, slices of radish and jicama, and a drizzle of the Avocado Crema. Serve warm.

Leftover fish and tortillas may be refrigerated in an airtight container for up to I week. Reheat, wrapped in a damp paper towel, in the microwave for 20 to 30 seconds per taco. The radishes and jicama may be covered in water and refrigerated, covered, for up to I week. The Avocado Crema may be refrigerated, covered, for 24 hours, but it should be used within the day.

SMOTHERED BURRITO
CHRISTMAS-STYLE

"Christmas style" is what folks in New Mexico say when they are referring to Mexican food smothered in a red and a green sauce. Red chile provides a smoky, earthy flavor, while green chile gives the dish a mild, roasted pepper taste. It's the best of both worlds! I always like to try a little of both. ★ This makes a festive dish for breakfast, lunch, or dinner.

serves 6

2 tablespoons olive oil

1 large potato, diced

1 pound lean ground beef, or ground turkey

¼ teaspoon salt

¼ teaspoon black pepper

¼ teaspoon cumin

4 large flour tortillas, (I recommend the type specifically made for burritos)

½ cup grated Oaxaca, or Monterey Jack cheese

1 cup Red Chile (recipe, p. 36)

1 cup Western Green Chile (recipe, p. 39)

Heat the olive oil in a medium skillet over medium heat. Add the diced potato and cook for 10 to 15 minutes, until it is fork-tender. Stir in the ground beef or turkey, the salt, black pepper, and cumin and continue cooking, stirring occasionally, for approximately 10 minutes, or until the meat is cooked through. Drain the meat mixture on a paper towel-lined plate.

Spoon the meat mixture and cheese down the middle of each tortilla, leaving about 1 inch of tortilla at each end of the filling. Fold each end over the filling, and then roll up the tortilla.

Arrange on a plate fold-side down, and top each burrito with ¼ cup Red Chile sauce and ¼ cup Western Green Chile sauce. Serve warm.

Leftover meat mixture, sauce, and tortillas may be refrigerated, in separate airtight containers for up to 1 week. Reheat the meat in a small skillet over medium heat for 5 minutes, or until heated through.

Wrap leftover tortillas in a damp paper towel and microwave for 15 to 20 seconds each. Heat the sauce in a small saucepan(s) over medium heat for 5 to 10 minutes, stirring occasionally.

FILET MIGNON
WITH CHIPOTLE PAN SAUCE

Pan-seared medallions of beef and a spicy pan sauce make a romantic dinner for two, but this recipe is really perfect for any special occasion. It's not too spicy, but turns up the heat just enough to let you know it hails from the Southwest. ★ *Serve with Hominy Au Gratin (recipe, p. 78), Baked Arroz with Green Chile and Roasted Garlic (recipe, p. 88), or fluffy mashed potatoes.*

serves 2

2 (10-ounce) filet mignon, 2-inches thick
1 tablespoon olive oil
1 tablespoon salt
1 tablespoon coarsely ground black pepper
3 tablespoons butter, room temperature, and divided
¾ cup red wine
1 chipotle pepper (canned, in adobo sauce), finely diced

Preheat the oven to 400° F.

Heat a cast-iron skillet on the stovetop on high heat for about 5 minutes.

Brush all sides of the filets with oil, and sprinkle with salt and pepper overall (this may seem like a generous amount of salt and pepper, but it's perfect for this thick cut of meat).

Place the filets in the dry, hot skillet and reduce the heat to medium-high. Sear for 1 to 2 minutes on each side, making sure to sear the outer edge of the filets as well. The seasoning will help form a crust on the meat.

Put 1 tablespoon butter atop each filet and place the skillet into the pre-heated oven to cook for 10 to 15 minutes. This will produce a medium-rare steak with an internal temperature of 120° to 125° F.

Transfer the filets to a serving plate and tent with foil. Allow the meat to rest for 10 to 15 minutes.

While the meat rests, return the skillet to the stovetop. Deglaze the pan over medium heat, whisking in the wine and scraping up all the browned bits left in the skillet. Add the remaining 1 tablespoon butter and the chipotle pepper. Reduce the heat to medium-low, and cook for 5 to 8 minutes to allow the wine to reduce by half.

Taste the sauce and add salt and pepper if desired. Plate the filets, spoon the pan sauce over each, and serve immediately.

Leftover filet can be refrigerated in an airtight container for up to 1 week. Slice the cold meat and toss in a salad for a delicious lunch.

CONFETTI FIDEOS

Fideos is a Spanish word for noodles. Fideos are usually short in length and thinner than spaghetti. It's also known as vermicelli. There are many preparations for fideos. This one was inspired by the goulash my mother makes. The noodles are toasted in a light amount of butter to give them an incredible, nutty flavor. ★ *This brightly colored dish is great for busy weeknights—it takes less than 30 minutes to prepare, from start to finish.*

serves 4 to 6

3 teaspoons olive oil, divided

1 pound ground turkey, or lean ground beef

1 tablespoon butter

8 ounces dry fideos, or vermicelli pasta

1 fresh jalapeño, stemmed, seeded, and finely diced

½ red bell pepper, stemmed, seeded, and diced

½ orange or yellow bell pepper, stemmed, seeded, and diced

½ Spanish onion, peeled and finely diced

Salt and black pepper, to taste

2 tablespoons tomato paste

½ cup grated Monterrey Jack cheese

¼ cup Spanish olives, sliced

2 tablespoons fresh cilantro leaves

Heat 1 ½ teaspoons olive oil in a large skillet over medium heat. Add ground turkey or beef and cook for 10 minutes, stirring occasionally, until the meat has browned. Drain the meat on a paper towel-lined plate.

Add the remaining 1 ½ teaspoons of oil to the same skillet, and melt the butter over medium heat. Once melted, add the noodles and toss to coat. Continue cooking over medium heat for 5 minutes, stirring often, until most of the noodles are toasted and lightly browned.

Add the jalapeño, red and yellow peppers, and onion, and stir to combine. Continue to cook for 5 minutes, until the peppers and onion are tender.

Return the meat to the skillet, season with a pinch of salt and pepper to taste, and stir to combine. Add 2 cups water and the tomato paste and whisk to incorporate. Reduce the heat to medium-low and simmer 4 to 5 minutes, until the noodles soften and absorb the water.

Remove from the heat and stir in the cheese, olives, and cilantro. Serve warm.

Leftovers can be refrigerated in an airtight container for up to 1 week. Reheat in a skillet over medium-low heat for 5 to 10 minutes.

STACKED ENCHILADAS
WITH RED CHILE

My uncle from New Mexico introduced us kids to a type of enchilada that we had never seen in west Texas. The layers of corn tortillas were stacked flat on top of each other with sauce, meat, cheese, and raw onion in between the layers. These certainly were not the rolled enchiladas we were used to; and the best part—he always put a fried egg on top! ★

serves 4

1 pound lean ground beef
1 teaspoon chili powder
½ teaspoon salt
¼ teaspoon black pepper
¼ teaspoon cumin
4 tablespoons vegetable oil, plus more for frying eggs
12 Handmade Corn Tortillas (recipe, p. 28)
1 to 2 cups Red Chile (recipe, p. 36)
4 eggs (optional)
½ Spanish onion, peeled and diced
1 cup grated cheddar cheese

Place the ground beef into a medium skillet over medium heat and stir in the chili powder, salt, black pepper, and cumin. Brown the beef 10 minutes, or until cooked through. Drain on a paper towel-lined plate.

Heat the oil in the same skillet over medium heat. Dip each tortilla into the oil, coating both sides, for about 2 or 3 seconds, just long enough to soften the tortilla. Place on a paper towel-lined tray.

Heat the Red Chile in a separate saucepan over medium heat for 5 minutes, until warm.

Add more oil as needed to fry the eggs (over-easy is recommended, but cook to your taste). Season with salt and pepper to taste.

Plate each stacked enchilada serving by layering a tortilla, the red chile, meat, cheese, and onion. Repeat twice more, using 3 tortillas per stack, and top with a fried egg. Serve immediately.

Leftover meat, tortillas, and the Red Chile can be refrigerated in separate airtight containers for up to 1 week. Reheat the meat in a small skillet over medium heat for 4 to 5 minutes. Heat the Red Chile in a small saucepan over medium heat for 5 minutes, or until heated through. Wrap leftover tortillas in a damp paper towel and reheat in the microwave for about 10 seconds each.

NOTE: Red Chile Sauce (recipe p. 40) may be substituted for Red Chile in this recipe.

GREEN CHILE CHICKEN ENCHILADAS

Creamy chicken enchiladas topped with green chile are a longtime favorite throughout Texas, and at my house. My daughter is an incredible cook and now the secret is out—this is her own recipe for these delectable enchiladas. ★ Serve with Anasazi Beans, (recipe, p. 80) and Spanish Rice (recipe, p. 81) for a true Tex-Mex experience.

serves 4 to 6

4 chicken breast halves, bone-in, skin on
4 tablespoons, plus 2 teaspoons olive oil
½ teaspoon crushed red pepper flakes
¼ teaspoon garlic powder
¼ teaspoon salt
I dozen Handmade Corn Tortillas (recipe,
   p. 28), or prepackaged corn tortillas
8 ounces light sour cream
I ½ cups grated cheddar-jack cheese

I ⅔ cups Western Green Chile (recipe,
   p. 39)

Toppings
I cup shredded Iceberg lettuce
I tomato, diced
¼ cup diced Spanish onion
¼ cup sliced black olives

Preheat the oven to 400° F.

Brush the chicken with 2 teaspoons olive oil and season with the red pepper flakes, garlic powder, and salt. Bake on a baking sheet for 30 to 35 minutes, until the juices run clear when pierced with a fork or knife. Set the chicken aside to cool. (Leave the oven turned on.)

Heat the remaining oil in a large skillet over medium heat. Dip the tortillas, one at a time, in the heated oil to soften them. (This will ensure that the tortillas roll up easily, and it will help the sauce cling to the tortilla.)

Once the chicken is cool enough to handle, remove the skin and debone the meat. Shred the chicken by hand and place into a medium mixing bowl. Stir in the sour cream and I cup grated cheese.

Pour ¼ of the Western Green Chile sauce into the bottom of a 9 x13-inch baking dish.

Fill each tortilla with 2 tablespoons of the chicken mixture, roll the tortilla up, and arrange in the baking dish atop the sauce. Top with the remaining sauce, then sprinkle with the remaining cheese.

Bake uncovered at 400° F for 15 minutes, until cheese is melted and mixture is bubbly.

Sprinkle the toppings evenly over the enchiladas and serve warm.

Leftovers may be refrigerated in an airtight container for up to I week. To reheat, let the enchiladas stand at room temperature for 30 minutes. Preheat the oven to 400° F, cover the baking dish with foil, and reheat for 20 minutes, or until heated through.

LAYERED RED ENCHILADAS

In the Southwest, we eat rolled enchiladas, stacked enchiladas, enchilada casserole—any form of enchilada, any day of the week. ★ *This one is lusciously gooey with cheese, so as a healthier option you may substitute ground turkey in place of beef.*

serves 4 to 6

1 tablespoon olive oil
1 Spanish onion, peeled and diced
1 glove garlic, peeled and minced
½ teaspoon salt
¼ teaspoon black pepper
1 ¼ pounds lean ground beef, or
   ground turkey
1 ½ cups grated colby-jack cheese
¾ cup grated cheddar cheese
1 ½ cups Red Chile Sauce, (recipe, p. 40)
12 Handmade Corn Tortillas (recipe,
   p. 28), or prepackaged corn tortillas
3 green onions, sliced
3 tablespoons fresh cilantro, chopped

Heat the olive oil in a large skillet over medium-high heat. Add the onion and garlic, season with salt and pepper, and cook 3 to 4 minutes, stirring occasionally. Add the ground beef or turkey, and stir well to combine. Continue cooking over medium heat for 5 minutes, until the meat has browned.

Preheat the oven to 350° F.

Combine the cheeses in a small bowl and set aside.

Spread ¼ cup Red Chile Sauce onto the bottom of a 9 x 13-inch baking dish. Tear 4 tortillas into halves and arrange in a single layer on top of the sauce, overlapping them as needed to cover the sauce. Top with 1 cup of the meat mixture, ⅓ of the remaining sauce, and ¾ cup cheese. Repeat the layers, ending with a cheese topping. Bake until the enchiladas are bubbly, about 30 minutes.

Top with green onions and fresh cilantro. Serve warm.

Leftovers may be refrigerated in an airtight container, or in the baking dish covered with foil, for up to 1 week. To reheat, allow the dish to come to room temperature for 30 minutes. Preheat the oven to 350° F and reheat, covered, for 20 minutes, or until heated through.

TEX-MEX BURGERS

Texans tend to turn any meal into a Southwestern meal. Adding green chiles gives most anything that special taste we desire. One of my aunts even carries green chiles in her purse to football games so she can add them to her hot dog. I once saw a friend pull out a baggie filled with green chiles from her purse in an elegant restaurant! But who am I to be surprised? I've been known to carry tortillas with me when I leave the state. ★ Try this burger at your next backyard barbeque and you may develop a Texas twang. Serve it with Fresh Fiesta Salad (recipe, p.82), or Anasazi Beans (recipe, p. 80). Yee haw!

serves 4

1 1/3 pound lean ground beef, or ground turkey

1 1/2 teaspoons salt, divided

1 teaspoon black pepper, divided

1 large sweet onion, such as Texas 1015, or Vidalia, peeled and sliced into rings

1 tablespoon grated piloncillo sugar, or brown sugar

2 tablespoons unsalted butter

2 whole fresh green chiles, such as Anaheim or New Mexico

4 slices Asadero cheese, or other mild cheese

2 tablespoons light mayonnaise

4 whole wheat hamburger buns

Divide the ground meat into 4 balls and flatten to form 4 patties. Season both sides of the patties with salt and black pepper, and set aside.

Prepare an outdoor grill to medium heat. (Both gas and charcoal work well.)

Place the onion slices in a piece of foil large enough to make a packet, and sprinkle sugar over them. Season with the remaining salt and black pepper, and top with butter. Fold and seal the foil to form a packet, leaving a small opening at the top.

Place the onion packet on the grill, cover, and cook for 20 minutes, checking once or twice to ensure the fire is not burning them. If they begin to blacken, place the packet further from the fire, or coals. Continue to cook the onions for another 30 minutes.

Place the green chiles on the grill and roast, turning, until the skins have blistered on all sides. Transfer the chiles to a small mixing bowl, cover tightly with plastic wrap, and set aside for 10 minutes. Next, remove and discard the blistered skins. Remove the stem, and slice the chiles open lengthwise. Remove and discard the seeds. Cut the chiles in half and set aside.

Place the meat patties on the grill, adding coal as needed to maintain a medium heat. Grill for 4 to 5 minutes on each side, to your desired doneness. Place 1 cheese slice on each burger, close the grill lid, and cook for another 1 to 2 minutes, or until the cheese begins to melt.

Toast the buns on the grill for 1 to 2 minutes.

Spread mayonnaise on the buns and add a meat patty, a slice of green chile, and a portion of caramelized onions, and enjoy.

Leftover burgers can be refrigerated in an airtight container for up to 1 week. Reheat the meat and buns separately in the microwave: heat the meat and green chiles for 30 to 45 seconds, and the buns for 10 to 15 seconds.

TACO CUPS

Eggroll and wonton wrappers can be used to hold a limitless array of delicious ingredients, much in the way we use tortillas and puff pastry. Serve these Taco Cups as appetizers, or as a main dish along with Fresh Yellow Squash Salad (recipe, p. 92), or Chili-Lime Cucumbers with Jicama (recipe, p. 84). ★ *A filling of Southwestern ingredients fuses Tex-Mex and Asian eggroll wrappers into a crunchy delight. Brush the wrapper with oil to help them crisp up in the oven, eliminating the need for deep frying. Stagger the wrappers in standard-size muffin tins, leaving every other cup empty to make room for the overhanging edges (see photo). You will need two tins with a total of 24 cups to accommodate 12 Taco Cups.*

yields 1 dozen

3 tablespoons olive oil, divided
1 small Spanish onion, peeled and diced
½ cup diced roasted green chiles (recipe, p. 38)
¼ teaspoon salt
¾ pound lean ground beef, or ground turkey
2 cups cooked rice
1 ½ cups Red Chile Sauce (recipe, p. 40)
12 eggroll wrappers, uncooked
½ cup grated colby-jack cheese

Toppings
Light sour cream
1 medium tomato, chopped
2 green onions, diced

Heat 1 ½ tablespoons oil in a large skillet over medium heat. Add the onion and green chiles, and sauté 5 minutes, stirring frequently, until the onion has softened. Add the salt, and ground beef or turkey, and continue cooking for 5 to 6 minutes until the meat is cooked through. Stir in the cooked rice and Red Chile Sauce.

Preheat the oven to 375° F. Place the muffin tins in the oven for 5 minutes to preheat, as well; this will allow the eggroll wrappers to cook more evenly.

Remove the tins from the oven and spray every other muffin cup with non-stick cooking spray. Brush both sides of each eggroll wrapper with the remaining 1 ½ tablespoons oil. Place the wrappers into the muffin cups that have been sprayed, pressing down lightly to line the cup.

Spoon equal portions of the meat and rice mixture into the eggroll-lined muffin cups, pressing to pack the mixture. Bake for 15 minutes, then remove from the oven and sprinkle equal portions of the grated cheese atop each taco cup. Continue baking for 3 to 5 minutes. When you are ready to serve, top with sour cream, tomatoes, and green onion, as desired. Serve warm.

Leftovers may be refrigerated in an airtight container for up to 1 week. Reheat on a baking sheet in a 375° F oven for 10 minutes.

BLACKENED CHICKEN TACOS

Inspired by the incredible flavors of blackened Cajun seafood, this recipe brings together a mouthwatering list of spices to make this an unforgettable taco. ★ *The meat is cooked over high heat, allowing the dry rub seasonings to combine and create an intense flavor. It is often cooked in a hot cast iron skillet, but this lighter grilled version will create the same flavor explosion.*

serves 4 to 6

Dry Rub

2 tablespoons chili powder

2 teaspoons cumin

2 teaspoons grated piloncillo sugar, or brown sugar

1 teaspoon salt

½ teaspoon black pepper

½ teaspoon Mexican oregano, or other dried oregano

½ teaspoon cinnamon

4 boneless, skinless chicken breast halves

2 tablespoons olive oil, plus 2 teaspoons for the tortillas

½ teaspoon salt

8 to 12 Handmade Flour Tortillas (recipe, p. 30), or Handmade Corn Tortillas (recipe, p. 28)

Mexican Crema with Lime (recipe, p. 23)

Prepare an outdoor grill, or heat a grill pan over medium-high heat for 5 minutes.

Mix the dry rub ingredients in a small bowl and set aside.

Brush both sides of the chicken breasts with a small amount of oil and season the bottom side with salt. Apply the dry rub to the top of the chicken breast, pressing with your fingertips to ensure the rub adheres to the chicken. Drizzle 2 tablespoons olive oil over the applied dry rub.

Place the chicken on the grill, dry-rub-side down over white-hot coals for 3 minutes. Or, if you are using a preheated grill pan, cook over medium-high heat for 3 minutes, or until the blackened side forms a crust. Gently turn the chicken over, cover, and continue to cook for 6 to 7 minutes, depending on the thickness of the chicken. The chicken is done if the juices run clear when pierced with a fork. Remove from the grill and allow the chicken to rest for a few minutes before thinly slicing.

Brush both sides of the tortillas with oil. Cook them on a grill or grill pan for 20 seconds per side, just long enough to lightly char each side.

Layer the tortillas with slices of chicken, Top with a drizzle of Mexican Crema with Lime. If you want additional toppings, choose the Three Amigos Pico de Gallo (recipe, p. 22), or Loaded Guacamole (recipe, p. 21).

Leftover chicken may be refrigerated in an airtight container for up to 1 week. Wrap in foil and reheat in a 350° F oven for 10 minutes.

SOUTHWESTERN SAUSAGE BUNDLES

I have a fantastic method for sausage making that doesn't require casings or special processing equipment. This type of sausage is best cooked and served immediately. It is not for preserving or freezing. A mixture of 50 percent venison and 50 percent pork is a great combination, if you can get fresh venison. I use this combo when my brother has been deer hunting. For the pork in this recipe, I ask the butcher to grind it ahead of time, which is a timesaver in the kitchen. ★ *Serve these with Hominy Au Gratin (recipe, p. 78), or Baked Arroz with Green Chile and Roasted Garlic (recipe, p. 88).*

serves 4 to 6

6 cornhusks (the kind used for making
    tamales), available in the produce
    section at most markets
2 pounds ground Boston Butt (pork
    shoulder)
I jalapeño, stemmed, seeded, and finely
    diced
½ red bell pepper, stemmed, seeded, and
    finely diced
I ½ teaspoons salt
I ½ teaspoons chili powder
I teaspoon garlic powder
I teaspoon onion powder
I teaspoon cumin
I teaspoon black pepper
I teaspoon crushed red pepper flakes
½ teaspoon smoked paprika

To prepare the cornhusks, fill the sink with warm water, separate the cornhusks, and submerge them in the water to soak for I hour, until they soften and become pliable.

In a mixing bowl, combine the ground pork with the jalapeño and bell pepper. Add the remaining seasonings to the pork mixture. With clean hands, blend the seasonings into the pork.

Divide the pork mixture into 6 equal pieces and shape them into sausages that are about 4 x 1 ¾- inches.

Blot the excess water from the cornhusks with a kitchen towel. Place I sausage on the center of each cornhusk and fold it up like a burrito. TIP: Use I additional cornhusk to tear or cut into "ribbons" to tie the bundles closed.

Heat a smoker to 125° to 130° F (many basic grills can also be used to "smoke" meats; check the manufacturer's instructions). Place the bundles directly into the smoker or grill and smoke for 2 hours. For the last 30 minutes, increase the heat source to achieve an internal temperature of 160° to 165° F, which is necessary for pork.

This last step can also be accomplished by baking the sausages in a 350° F oven for 15 to 20 minutes.

If the husks begin to turn very brown or to burn, wrap the bundles in foil. This will not allow as much smoke to treat the sausages, but better safe than sorry.

Leftover sausage bundles can be wrapped in foil and refrigerated for up to I week. Reheat in a preheated 350° F oven for about 10 minutes.

RANCHERS' CHILAQUILES CASSEROLE

Chilaquiles is a Mexican dish made with crispy pieces of corn tortillas topped with a sauce that softens the tortillas. It is similar to "migas", another dish that contains torn pieces of tortilla. ★ *Chilaquiles is often served for breakfast, same as migas. But this hardy casserole serves as a main dish any time of day.*

serves 6

3 boneless, skinless chicken breast halves

1 teaspoon olive oil

1 teaspoon salt, divided

¼ teaspoon black pepper

¼ teaspoon crushed red pepper flakes

¼ teaspoon dried Mexican oregano, or
    other oregano

5 tablespoons vegetable oil

1 small Spanish onion, peeled and diced

1 jalapeño, stemmed, seeded, and finely
    diced

2 tablespoons all-purpose flour

2 tablespoons chili powder

½ teaspoon cumin

2 cups chicken broth

½ cup milk

2 ½ cups crushed Fresh Corn Tortilla
    Chips, (recipe, p. 20)

1 ½ cups grated colby-jack cheese

Topping

4 green onions, cleaned and sliced

1 tomato, diced

Preheat the oven to 400° F.

Lightly brush the chicken breasts with olive oil, and season with a mixture of ¼ teaspoon salt, the black pepper, red pepper flakes, and oregano. Place the breasts in a baking dish and bake for 25 to 35 minutes, until the juices run clear when pierced with a fork. Let the chicken cool slightly, then shred by hand.

Reduce the oven heat to 350° F.

Heat the vegetable oil in a large skillet over medium heat. Add the onion, jalapeño, and the remaining salt, and sauté for 5 minutes, until the onion is transparent.

Whisk the flour into the skillet and continue to whisk for 30 seconds, until the flour browns. Add the chili powder and cumin, and stir to combine. Add the chicken broth and milk, and whisk to combine. Continue cooking over medium heat for 1 minute, whisking occasionally, until the mixture thickens. Stir in the shredded chicken and remove from the heat and set aside.

Add ½ of the crushed tortilla chips to the bottom of a 9 x 13-inch baking dish. Pour ½ the chicken mixture over the crushed chips and top with ½ the grated cheese. Repeat the layers. Bake the casserole at 350° F for 20 minutes until the cheese is melted and the mixture is bubbly.

Top with a sprinkling of the onions and tomatoes and serve warm.

Leftovers may be refrigerated in an airtight container, or in a baking dish covered with foil, for up to 1 week. To reheat, let the dish sit at room temperature for 30 minutes. Preheat the oven to 350° F, and cook, covered, for 20 minutes, or until heated through.

REAL TAMALE PIE

Tamale pie is a simple way to enjoy the taste of tamales without as much work in the kitchen. ★ *I like to serve this pie with Spanish rice (recipe, p. 81), a fresh tossed salad, or Slow-Cooker Black Beans (recipe, p. 93).*

serves 6

1 to 1 ¼ pounds pork tenderloin, silver skin removed and discarded
½ teaspoon salt
¼ teaspoon black pepper
1 teaspoon olive oil
2 Guajillo, or New Mexico dried red chile pods
2 cloves garlic, peeled and smashed

Sauce
2 Roma tomatoes, cut into halves
2 tomatillos, husks removed, and halved
1 Spanish onion, peeled and halved
1 cup of reserved cooking liquid
½ teaspoon cumin
½ teaspoon dried oregano
½ teaspoon salt

Masa
1 cup masa harina, found in most supermarkets near the all-purpose flour
⅓ cup vegetable shortening, plus 1 teaspoon to grease pan
½ cup remaining reserved cooking liquid
½ teaspoon baking powder
½ teaspoon salt

1 cup grated cheddar cheese

To remove the pork's silver skin, slip your fingertips under the loose edge of the skin and pull back until you meet resistance. Slip the point of a small sharp knife under the remaining skin and run the knife blade between the tenderloin and the silver skin, pulling the silver skin back with your other hand as you go. The silver skin continues between the tenderloin and a thin, white fat cap. Continue sliding the blade to remove the cap and remaining silver skin.

Season the pork with salt and pepper. Heat the oil in a large skillet over medium-high heat, and sear all sides of the pork, 1 minute per side.

Clean the chile pods with a damp paper towel. Split the pods with a paring knife, and remove the seeds and stems.

Place the pork in a slow-cooker with the dried chiles, garlic, and 1 ½ cups water. Cook on high for 3 to 4 hours, or on low for 6 to 7 hours. Reserve the cooking liquid, adding water or broth as needed to reach 1 ½ cups (for the sauce and the masa). Set the meat aside to cool. When it has cooled enough to handle, dice the meat into fine pieces and place in a medium mixing bowl.

To make the sauce, preheat the oven to 425° F.

Spread the tomatoes, tomatillos, and onion halves cut side down on a baking sheet and roast them 15 to 20 minutes, or until the edges of the vegetables begin to blister and brown. Set aside. Turn the oven down to 350° F.

Pour 1 cup of the reserved liquid into a blender along with the roasted tomatoes, tomatillos and onion, and add the cumin, oregano, and salt. Pulse on medium speed until blended and smooth. Pour this sauce into the bowl with the diced pork and fold to coat the meat.

To make the masa, combine all the masa ingredients in a medium mixing bowl and work with your hands until the mixture comes together to make a dough ball. Place the dough ball in a 9-inch springform pan, greased with shortening, and pat the dough flat using your knuckles. Use the back of a spoon to spread it to the sides of the pan. (See the how-to on page 122 for detailed instructions.)

Spoon the pork filling onto the masa dough. Cover the pan tightly with foil (to help steam the masa). Bake at 350° F for 30 minutes. Carefully remove the foil and continue baking for another 30 minutes. Sprinkle the cheese evenly over the top of the pie, and continue to bake another 10 minutes.

Allow the pie to rest at room temperature for 10 minutes before removing the ring from the springform pan. Cut into wedges and serve warm.

HOW TO MAKE REAL TAMALE PIE MASA

1.
You will need a 9-inch springform pan, greased with shortening

2.
Cut shortening into the masa harina, baking powder, and salt with a pastry cutter or 2 butter knives

3.
Add cooking liquid to dough

4.
Stir mixture until well combined

5.
Gather into a dough ball

6.
Press the dough into the bottom of the greased pan creating a 1/2-inch lip around the sides.
Add the filling and bake.

CHICKEN VERDE TAMALES

Many folks in the Southwest couldn't imagine a Christmas meal without these tamales. It's popular for family members to get together to make this treat, each one responsible for a particular step in the process. When a group comes together to make tamales, the event is referred to as a tamalada, and it is about so much more than assembling tamales. It's about the family enjoying their time together, and paying tribute to those who have come before them, and passing the tradition to a new generation. ⭐

yields 3 dozen

Tamale Filling
5 pounds chicken (chicken breasts and thighs), bone-in, skin-on
I teaspoon salt
I teaspoon black pepper
I head garlic, cloves separated, peeled and smashed
5 tomatillos, husked
2 jalapeños, stemmed
3 tablespoons fresh lemon juice
Zest of I lemon

Masa
5 cups masa harina, available at most supermarkets near the all-purpose flour
2 ½ teaspoons baking powder
I ½ teaspoons salt
I ²/3 cups vegetable shortening
5 cups reserved cooking broth

3 dozen dried cornhusks, available at most supermarkets

Place the chicken in a large slow cooker. Sprinkle with salt and pepper, and stir in the garlic. Add I ½ quarts water, cover, and cook on high for 4 hours.

After 4 hours, add the tomatillos, jalapeños, lemon juice, and lemon zest. Continue cooking on high for 30 to 40 minutes, until the tomatillos and jalapeños are tender.

Use a slotted spoon to transfer the chicken to a cutting board to cool enough to handle.

Place the broth, along with the tomatillos and jalapeños, into a blender. Pulse on medium speed until the broth is chunky and the jalapeños have broken into small bits.

Discard the skins from the chicken and debone the meat. Finely shred the chicken and place it into a medium mixing bowl with I ½ cups of the blended broth.

In a separate large mixing bowl, combine the masa harina, baking powder, and salt. Add 5 cups of the blended broth and stir until well combined.

With an electric mixer, beat the shortening on medium speed for 2 minutes, until light and fluffy. Add the masa mixture to the bowl of the mixer and mix on low speed until well combined. The mixture will be slightly sticky and resemble the consistency of peanut butter.

To prepare the cornhusks, fill the sink with warm water, separate the corn husks, and submerge them in the water to soak for I hour, until they soften and become pliable.

Drain the husks and pat them dry with a kitchen towel. The husks should be no wider than 4 inches at the widest end. If the husk is too wide, tear or cut off the excess.

Working with a batch of I dozen, find the smooth side of each husk. With the back of a large tablespoon or small spatula, spread a thin layer of masa onto the smooth side of the corn husk, about 1/8-inch thick. Spread side to side, starting at the top (the wide end), and spreading downward about 5 inches.

Fill each one with 2 tablespoons of the chicken mixture, spreading it lengthwise

down the middle of the husk. Fold the left side of the husk over the filling, and then fold the right side over it. Secure by grasping the tail end of the corn husk and folding it up over the seam of the husk.

When you have finished rolling all the tamales, place them in the slow cooker filled with 1 ½ inches of the remaining broth mixture to steam. Stand the tamales open-end up and fill the pot tightly so the tamales cannot fall over. TIP: You can also set a cup in the center of the cooker to take up space or to lean the tamales on. Cover and cook the tamales on high for 4 hours. When you remove the tamales, the masa will set up almost immediately and become firm.

Serve warm. If you aren't planning to eat them immediately, wrap in foil, 1 dozen per foil packet, and refrigerate up to 1 week. To reheat the tamales, place them in a microwave-safe baking dish and top with a wet kitchen towel to allow the tamales to steam. Microwave on high in 1 minutes intervals until they are heated through.

NOTE: The chicken mixture and masa can be refrigerated separately in airtight containers for 2 to 3 days ahead if you wish.

GULF COAST STREET TACOS
WITH RAINBOW SESAME SLAW

Contrary to popular belief, not everything in Texas is big. Food trucks around town offer a variety of tacos and Mexican fare in perfect small portions, convenient for lunch or for a snack. Gulf Coast Street Tacos is the perfect meal for you and your family and friends while standing around a barbeque pit. ★ *Pair them with Calabacitas (recipe, p. 85), or Mexican Street Corn (recipe, p. 86), a cold beverage, and the wide-open sky.*

serves 6

½ red bell pepper, stemmed, seeded, and julienned

½ orange bell pepper, stemmed, seeded, and julienned

½ yellow bell pepper, stemmed, seeded, and julienned

I jalapeño pepper, stemmed, seeded, and julienned

¼ head purple cabbage, sliced into thin ribbons

4 tablespoons fresh lime juice

2 tablespoons honey

I tablespoon sesame oil

¼ teaspoon salt

I pound shrimp, peeled and deveined

2 tablespoons olive oil

12 Handmade Corn Tortillas (recipe, p. 28)

In a medium mixing bowl, toss together the bell peppers, jalapeño, and cabbage.

In a separate small bowl, whisk together the lime juice, honey, sesame oil, and salt. Pour this mixture over the peppers and cabbage and stir to coat the slaw.

Prepare an outdoor grill, or preheat a cast-iron grill pan over medium-high heat for 5 minutes.

Brush the shrimp with olive oil and thread them onto skewers. Carefully place the skewered shrimp on the grill, or a preheated grill pan over medium heat, and cook I to 2 minutes on each side, or until the shrimp turn pink and opaque.

Place the tortillas onto a grill or grill pan, and lightly char, about 20 seconds on each side.

Build each taco, placing 3 or 4 shrimp onto each tortilla and topping them with a portion of the slaw. Fold the tortilla over and serve warm, or at room temperature.

Leftover slaw can be covered with plastic wrap and refrigerated for 3 to 4 days. Extra shrimp and tortillas can be refrigerated in airtight containers for up to 3 or 4 days. Reheat the shrimp and tortillas, wrapped in a damp paper towel, in the microwave for 20 seconds per taco.

NAVAJO TACOS

Navajo Tacos are made with Indian fry bread. The fried bread creates a vessel for taco ingredients and is common among many Southwestern Native American Indian tribes. ★ The dough for the base of the taco is deep fried. Substituting vegetable oil for lard, which was originally used to fry the bread, doesn't take away any flavor. These are very filling, so I usually serve 1 taco per person. Other lettuces with more nutritional value may be used instead, but I like the iceberg lettuce because its high water content provides a crispy freshness.

serves 4

Fry Bread

2 cups all-purpose flour, plus more
  for dusting
1 teaspoon baking powder
1 teaspoon salt
1 cup milk
4 cups vegetable oil, or enough for a
  depth of 1 ½ inches

2 tablespoons olive oil
1 large potato, diced
1 pound lean ground beef, or
  ground turkey
¼ teaspoon salt
¼ teaspoon black pepper
¼ teaspoon cumin
4 cups shredded iceberg lettuce
1 tomato, diced
2 tablespoons minced onion
¼ cup grated cheddar cheese

Light sour cream
Charred Salsa (recipe, p. 41)

Stir the flour, baking powder, and salt together in a medium mixing bowl. Add the milk and stir to combine. Turn the dough out onto a floured surface and knead for 5 minutes. Divide into 4 balls and let them rest for 5 minutes.

Heat enough oil to reach a depth of 1 ½ inches in a deep skillet, (or other pan suitable for frying) over medium-high heat. Using a deep fry thermometer, wait for the temperature to rise to 365° F.

Use your hand to flatten each ball into a disk, ¼-inch thick, and press a dimple with your thumbs in the center of the disk (see photo). Fry one taco at a time, 2 or 3 minutes on each side, until golden brown. Drain on a paper towel-lined plate.

Heat the olive oil in a separate medium skillet over medium heat. Add the diced potato and cook for 10 to 15 minutes, until it is fork-tender. Add the ground beef or turkey, salt, black pepper, and cumin. Continue cooking, stirring occasionally, for 10 minutes, or until the meat is cooked through. Drain the mixture on a paper towel-lined plate.

To build the Navajo Taco, divide the meat mixture, lettuce, tomato, onion, and cheese between each fry bread. Top with Charred Salsa and a dollop of light sour cream, as desired, and serve warm.

The leftover meat mixture and fry bread can be refrigerated in an airtight container for up to 1 week. Reheat the meat in a small skillet over medium heat for 5 minutes, or until heated through. The fry bread can be reheated, one at a time, in the microwave for 15 to 20 seconds each.

ROASTED PORK LOIN
WITH MOLE AMARILLO

Mole is a mix of chiles, spices, and nuts, and can contain a wide variety of other ingredients. Many popular versions of mole contain chocolate. Or, it can simply consist of whatever types of ingredients are readily available. ★ *According to legend, early in the colonial period the Convent of Santa Rosa in Puebla was to be paid a visit by the area archbishop. The poor nuns lived a meager lifestyle and went into a tailspin trying to decide what to feed the archbishop. After they said their prayers, they gathered what they had on hand—chile peppers, spices, nuts, breadcrumbs, and chocolate—which they mixed together to create a delicious sauce. They cooked a turkey and poured the mole sauce over the pieces of turkey. Naturally, the archbishop loved the spicy creation, and you will, too!*

serves 8 to 10

Mole

5 dried Guajillo or New Mexico chiles

¼ teaspoon achiote or annatto seeds, found in most supermarkets, or online

1 stick canela (a thin, flaky Mexican cinnamon), or substitute 1 teaspoon cinnamon

1 clove

¼ teaspoon cumin seeds

¼ teaspoon dried Mexican oregano, or other oregano

2 tablespoons olive oil, divided

6 cloves garlic, peeled, and smashed

1 Spanish onion, peeled and diced

4 tomatillos, husks removed and quartered

2 yerbar leaves, found in most supermarkets, or online

⅓ cup masa harina, found in most supermarkets near the all-purpose flour

½ teaspoon salt

½ cup pinon (pine) nuts

(Continued on page 132)

Clean the dried chiles with a damp paper towel. Use a paring knife to split them open lengthwise, and remove the stems and seeds. Heat a cast iron skillet over medium heat and toast the chiles for about 1 minute on each side. Remove the skillet from the stove and add 2 cups hot water to soften the chiles. Add the achiote seeds and let them soak for 20 minutes. Remove the chiles and seeds and set aside. Reserve the soaking liquid.

Using a mortar and pestle, or an electric spice mill, grind the canela, clove, cumin seeds, and oregano together and set aside.

Heat 1 tablespoon oil in a small skillet over medium heat. Sauté the garlic and onion for 5 minutes, stirring often, until tender. Add the tomatillos and continue to cook until soft.

In an electric blender, combine the chiles, achiote seeds, ground spices, garlic, onion, tomatillos, yerbar leaves, masa harina, salt, and 1/2 cup of the reserved soaking liquid. Pulse on medium speed until the mixture is smooth. Strain the mixture into a medium mixing bowl, pushing the mixture through a strainer with a wooden spoon or rubber spatula. Add the portion that sticks to the bottom of the strainer into the bowl, as well. Return the mixture to the blender. Discard the skins of the chiles left in the strainer.

Toast the pinion nuts, pepitas, and sesame seeds in a dry skillet over medium heat for about 1 minute, or until they turn golden brown. Stir often to ensure they do not burn. Add the toasted nuts and seeds to the mixture in the blender and blend on medium speed until a thick paste forms. If it is too thick, add 1 or 2 tablespoons of the reserved soaking liquid to thin it; the consistency should be similar to mashed potatoes.

Heat the remaining 1 tablespoon oil in a large skillet over medium heat.

(Continued on page 132)

ROASTED PORK LOIN *(Continued)*

½ cup pepitas (pumpkin seeds)
1 tablespoon sesame seeds
1 ½ cups chicken broth

Pork Loin
2 (10- to 12-ounce) pork loins, silver
   skin removed and discarded
1 tablespoon olive oil
1 tablespoon smoked paprika
1 teaspoon dried thyme
1 teaspoon pumpkin pie spice
1 teaspoon salt
1 teaspoon coarsely ground black pepper
¼ teaspoon cayenne

Cilantro leaves, for garnish

Spoon the paste into the skillet and reduce heat to medium-low, letting it brown for about 30 minutes, turning and stirring often. The thick base for the mole needs to brown, or "toast" in the skillet, which will add a nutty flavor before thinning it with broth.

Stir the chicken broth into the paste to thin it, and cook 5 more minutes, stirring often. This will create a thick sauce.

Preheat oven to 450 degrees F.

To make the pork: Remove the pork loin's silver skin. Slip your fingertips under the loose edge of the skin and pull back until you meet resistance. Slip the point of a small sharp knife under the remaining skin and run the knife blade between the tenderloin and the silver skin, pulling the silver skin back with your other hand as you go. The silver skin continues between the tenderloin and a thin, white fat cap. Continue sliding the blade to remove the cap and remaining silver skin.

Brush the pork loins with oil and place them on a baking sheet.

In a small bowl, combine all the spices and rub them evenly over all the pork.

Roast the pork loins for 25 minutes, then remove from the oven and allow them to rest at room temperature for 5 minutes before slicing. Pour the sauce over the pork medallion, garnish with cilantro, and serve warm.

Leftover pork may be refrigerated in an airtight container for up to 1 week. To reheat, wrap the meat in foil, and bake in a preheated 350° F oven for 15 to 20 minutes. Extra mole sauce can be refrigerated in an airtight container for up to 1 week, as well. Reheat the sauce in a saucepan over medium heat for 5 minutes, or until heated through. Mole, in the paste stage, may also be frozen, then thawed and reheated. Thin it with broth as needed when reheating.

JACQUELINE'S CHILE BRAISED BEEF

Although my husband, Michael, didn't grow up with lots of traditional Mexican food in his home, his mother, Jacqueline, did wonders with freshly ground red chiles. I never had the pleasure of knowing her, but Jacqueline was a lovely Southern woman who made many delicious meals. Michael recalls that she served these chile braised cubes of beef over fried potatoes, which were probably cooked in a cast-iron skillet. ★ *This dish is also delicious served over steamed rice. Either way, it is one of Michael's all-time favorites. His mom's might have been better, but I think I hit a homerun with this recipe.*

serves 4

5 tablespoons all-purpose flour, divided
1 ½ teaspoons salt, divided
½ teaspoon garlic powder
½ teaspoon onion powder
½ teaspoon black pepper, divided
1 ½ pounds beef sirloin, trimmed and
  cut into bite-size cubes
5 tablespoons shortening, divided
¼ cup chili powder
¼ teaspoon dried Mexican oregano, or
  other oregano
¼ teaspoon cumin
¼ cup vegetable oil
4 Russet potatoes, cleaned, peeled, and
  diced

Mix 2 tablespoons flour, ½ teaspoon salt, the garlic powder, onion powder, and ¼ teaspoon black pepper in a shallow dish. Toss the cubed beef in the flour mixture to coat.

Melt 2 tablespoons shortening in a large skillet over medium-high heat. Sear half of the floured beef cubes over medium-high heat for 1 minute on all sides, until the meat is browned. Remove with a slotted spoon and drain on a paper towel-lined plate. Melt 1 more tablespoon shortening in the skillet and repeat the process with the remaining beef.

To make the braising sauce, reduce the heat to medium and add the remaining shortening to the skillet. Whisk in the remaining flour and stir for 1 to 2 minutes, until the mixture is golden in color. Stir in the chili powder, ½ teaspoon salt, oregano, and cumin. Slowly add 2 cups water, whisking constantly until well blended.

Add the seared beef to the sauce and simmer over medium low heat for 30 minutes, stirring occasionally.

While the meat braises, heat the oil over medium heat in a cast-iron skillet. Test the heat of the oil by dropping 1 piece of potato into the skillet; when it sizzles, add the rest. Season with ½ teaspoon salt and ¼ teaspoon black pepper, and cook for 15 minutes, stirring occasionally, or until the potatoes are golden brown and tender. Use a slotted spoon to transfer the potatoes to a paper towel-lined plate to drain.

When ready to serve, spoon the braised beef and braising sauce over the fried potatoes.

Leftover beef and potatoes may be refrigerated in separate airtight containers for up to 1 week. Reheat the beef and braising sauce in a skillet over medium-low heat for 10 to 15 minutes, or until the meat is heated through. Reheat the potatoes in a microwave-safe dish in a microwave in 20 second intervals, until heated through.

AVOCADO TORTA

Torta is the Spanish, Portuguese, and Italian word for flatbread. It is also the word used for a Mexican sandwich. The sandwiches, or "tortas", are often made on a white, crusty, Mexican bread called "bolillos." Hoagie rolls make a suitable substitute, and better yet, a good whole grain, crusty bread would be perfect for building this sandwich that is reminiscent of a lighter BLT. ★ *So many of us love anything with avocado, and the notable health benefits make this dish that much better.*

yields 2 tortas

¼ pound Serrano ham, thinly sliced

½ Haas avocado, pitted, and skin removed

3 tablespoons light mayonnaise

¼ teaspoon chili powder, or more if you prefer the heat

2 bolillo rolls, or 1 (12-inch) hoagie roll, cut in half

2 large leaves green leaf lettuce, rinsed and dried

4 tomato slices

Salt and black pepper to taste

In a small skillet, brown the Serrano ham over medium heat for 2 to 3 minutes, until it begins to crisp. Drain the ham on a paper towel-lined plate and gently press the top with another paper towel to remove the excess grease.

Slice the avocado half into ½-inch slices, lengthwise.

Mix the mayo and chili powder together in a small dish.

If you desire, you may toast the bread halves in a toaster, or on a baking sheet under a preheated broiler for 3 to 5 minutes.

Divide the chili-mayo between each piece of bread, and spread it with a knife.

Layer the lettuce, 2 tomato slices, half the ham slices, and half the avocado slices onto each sandwich. Season with salt, pepper and chili powder to taste.

This is a nice sandwich to pack for lunch, but be sure to keep it chilled since it contains mayonnaise.

CHICKEN TINGA TACOS

Tinga is a Mexican dish with shredded beef or shredded chicken, and it has been my son's favorite for years. One of my biggest pleasures in life is feeding my family a nutritious, delicious meal they love. My son is all grown up now, but I will still drop everything and make this dish for him, anytime. ★

serves 4 to 6

4 chicken breast halves, bone-in, skin-on
I teaspoon salt
½ teaspoon black pepper
¼ teaspoon crushed red pepper flakes
¼ cup olive oil
4 garlic cloves, peeled and minced
I (28-ounce) can whole tomatoes, with juice
2 to 3 chipotle peppers (canned, in adobo sauce), finely diced
8 to 12 Handmade Corn Tortillas (recipe, p. 28) or Handmade Flour Tortillas (recipe, p. 30)

Optional Toppings
Light sour cream
Grated Monterrey Jack cheese

Preheat oven to 375° F.

Season the chicken with salt, black pepper, and red pepper flakes. Heat the oil in a Dutch oven over medium-high heat, and sear the chicken about 2 minutes per side, until all sides are light brown. Cover the chicken and bake for 45 minutes.

Remove the chicken from the Dutch oven, reserving the drippings, and transfer the chicken to a cutting board to cool slightly. When the chicken is cool enough to handle, discard the skin and debone the chicken, setting the meat aside.

Place the Dutch oven with the drippings over medium heat and add the garlic, tomatoes with juice, and chipotle peppers. Using a handheld potato masher, break the tomatoes up a bit. Stir in the deboned chicken, and simmer for 30 minutes.

Spoon a portion of the chicken into warm corn or flour tortillas and top with light sour cream and grated Monterey Jack cheese, as desired. Serve warm.

Refrigerate leftovers in an airtight container for up to I week. Reheat the leftovers in a skillet over medium heat for 10 to 15 minutes, adding I to 2 tablespoons water, as needed.

DULCES

Desserts with a sweet tooth

MINI TRES LECHES CAKES
WITH ALMOND BRITTLE

Tres leches cake is a sponge cake that is soaked in three types of milk. It is typically topped with sweetened whipped cream and is a favorite dessert at celebrations all over the Southwest. ★ *Smaller versions of the cake that look like mini Bundt cakes make a pretty presentation and may be soaked in the milk mixture individually as you prepare to serve them.*

yields 12 to 15 mini-cakes

1 cup all-purpose flour
2 teaspoons baking powder
¼ teaspoon salt
1 cup sugar
¾ cup unsalted butter, softened,
   plus more to grease the tins
3 eggs, room temperature
1 cup sweetened condensed milk
1 cup almond milk
1 cup evaporated milk

Topping
½ cup heavy whipping cream
2 tablespoons powdered sugar

Almond Brittle
1 tablespoon unsalted butter
⅓ cup light brown sugar
⅓ cup sliced almonds

Preheat the oven to 350° F. Lightly grease a non-stick mini-cake tin (about the size of a standard cupcake) with butter.

In a medium mixing bowl, sift together the flour, baking powder, and salt. Set aside.

With an electric mixer, cream the sugar and butter on medium speed for 3 to 4 minutes, until it is light and fluffy. Scrape down the sides of the bowl with a rubber spatula. With the mixer running, add the eggs, one at a time, until the mixture is smooth. Gently fold the dry ingredients into the wet ingredients until just combined.

Spoon or pipe the batter into the prepared mini-cake tin cups, filling each halfway full. Tap the bottom of the pan on a countertop to settle the batter. Bake for 12 to 15 minutes. When a toothpick inserted into one of the cakes comes out clean, they are done. Let the cakes cool in the tins for a few minutes, then gently slide a butter knife around the edges to lift each cake out. Transfer the cakes to a wire rack to continue cooling.

In a medium mixing bowl, combine the three milks and set aside.

With an electric mixer, whip the heavy cream until soft peaks form. Add the powdered sugar and whip for another 30 to 60 seconds.

To make the Almond Brittle, melt the butter in a small skillet over medium heat. Stir in the brown sugar and 1 tablespoon water, and in a few seconds it will begin to bubble. At that point, reduce the heat to medium-low and add the almonds, stirring to coat. Cook for 1 to 2 minutes. Spoon the brittle onto a parchment paper-lined tray to cool. Then crumble the brittle into chunks.

Plate the mini-cakes and pour about 3 tablespoons of the milk mixture over each cake. The milk will pool around the cake, then begin to be absorbed. When it is partially absorbed, top each cake with a dollop of whipped cream and a few crumbs of brittle and serve.

Store any un-soaked cakes and brittle in airtight containers for 3 to 4 days. The leftover milk mixture and the whipped cream may be cover and refrigerated for 3 to 4 days.

BUTTERY RUM BANANAS, MANGOS, AND PINEAPPLE

If you're a fan of Bananas Foster, you're going to love this sautéed mix of tropical fruit. Serve it as is, or topped with Cinnamon Ice Cream (recipe, p. 151). ★ *If you enjoy cooking outdoors, this one is nice to make right on the barbecue in a grill-safe skillet.*

serves 4

4 tablespoons unsalted butter

²/₃ cup light brown sugar

¼ cup light rum

1 ½ teaspoons Mexican vanilla, or other vanilla extract

½ teaspoon cinnamon

2 bananas, peeled and cut in ½-inch slices

1 mango, diced (see how-to, p. 34)

4 (½-inch) round slices fresh pineapple

In a large skillet over medium heat, melt the butter and stir in the brown sugar, rum, vanilla, and cinnamon. The mixture will begin to bubble within a few seconds. Cook, stirring constantly, for 1 minute.

Add the bananas and mangos, and stir to coat. Push the bananas and mangos to one side of the skillet and add the pineapple slices. Spoon the buttery rum sauce over the pineapple slices, and continue cooking for 1 to 2 minutes.

For each serving, scoop 1 pineapple slice into a serving bowl and top with a portion of bananas and mangos. Add a scoop of Cinnamon Ice Cream, if desired. Serve warm or at room temperature.

Leftover fruit may be refrigerated in an airtight container for 2 to 3 days. Reheat leftovers in a skillet over medium heat for 1 to 2 minutes.

COCONUT EMPANADAS

An empanada is a baked or fried pastry popular in Latin America as well as the Southwest. They can be filled with either a savory or a sweet filling, like this one. ★

yields 10

Filling

^{1}/3 cup sweetened shredded
 coconut

¾ cup sugar

3 cups whole milk, divided

4 egg yolks

¼ cup cornstarch

1 tablespoon unsalted butter

1 teaspoon Mexican vanilla, or
 other vanilla extract

Dough

2 ^{1}/3 cups all-purpose flour, plus
 more for dusting

½ teaspoon salt

4 ounces cream cheese, softened

½ cup butter, softened

½ cup cold shortening

1 egg, beaten

1 tablespoon milk or water

Preheat the oven to 325° F.

Spread the coconut evenly in a single layer on a baking sheet. Toast in the preheated oven for 5 minutes, then stir and continue to cook another 3 to 5 minutes until the coconut is a golden brown color. Remove and set aside to cool.

Combine the sugar and 2 ¾ cups milk in a medium saucepan over medium heat. Bring to a slow boil. This will take 3 to 4 minutes, then reduce the heat to low.

In a small mixing bowl, whisk together the remaining milk, egg yolks, and cornstarch until smooth. Temper the egg yolk mixture by whisking in a small amount of the warm milk to bring up the temperature of the eggs.

Gradually add the egg mixture to the saucepan, whisking until combined. Raise the heat to medium. Bring the mixture to a slow boil again, and cook for 3 minutes, stirring constantly, until the mixture has thickened.

Remove the saucepan from the heat and stir in the butter, vanilla, and coconut until well combined. Set aside to cool.

To prepare the dough, preheat the oven to 375° F.

In a small mixing bowl, sift together the flour and salt.

With an electric mixer, or a food processor equipped with a stainless steel mixing blade, mix the cream cheese and butter until well blended. Gradually add in the flour and salt mixture. Then add the cold shortening and mix until the dough comes together.

Turn the dough out onto a well-floured surface and use your floured hands to form a round disk. Roll the dough out with a lightly floured rolling pin to a ⅛- to ¹/16-inch thickness. I typically cut the dough into 5-inch diameter circles using a small saucer as a template. (If you make smaller circles, you don't have much room for the filling.) Re-roll the remaining dough, being cautious not to overwork it, and cut the remaining circles.

Place the circles of dough on 2 parchment-lined baking sheets. Spoon approximately 3 tablespoons coconut filling onto each circle of dough.

Beat the egg in a small bowl with 1 tablespoon milk, or water. Brush the edges of the dough with egg mixture to act as a glue to help seal the dough. Fold the dough over the filling to form a half-circle and crimp the edges of the dough, using your thumb and forefinger, or the tines of a fork to seal. Cut 3 small slits in the top of each empanada to allow steam to escape. Brush the tops with the remaining egg mixture, and bake for 20 to 25 minutes, until the crust is golden brown.

TARTA DE QUESO

Tarta de Queso is a Mexican cheesecake. This one has a tangy lime flavor and a hint of cinnamon in the crust, topped off with a beautiful garnish of candied lime slices. ★ *It's a perfect dessert for a Sunday dinner, and is so popular at our house, it is often requested by my son and husband for their birthday celebrations.*

serves 8

Filling
24 ounces cream cheese, softened
1 stick (½ cup) unsalted butter, softened
1 cup sugar
2 eggs
Zest of 1 lime
3 tablespoons fresh lime juice

Crust
⅓ cup unsalted butter, melted
1 ¼ cup graham cracker crumbs
3 tablespoons sugar
½ teaspoon cinnamon

Garnish
2 limes, seeded and thinly sliced
1 ¼ cup sugar, divided

In the bowl of an electric mixer, whip the cream cheese for 30 to 60 seconds, until it is smooth and fluffy. Add the butter and whip 1 minute, or until smooth and creamy. Scrape down the sides of the bowl. Add the sugar and eggs and beat on medium speed until well combined. Add the lime zest and lime juice and beat until incorporated.

Preheat the oven to 400° F.

To make the crust, combine the melted butter, graham cracker crumbs, sugar, and cinnamon in a small mixing bowl. Press the crumb mixture into a 9-inch springform pan to cover the bottom and sides of the pan.

Spoon the batter into the crust and spread evenly. Jiggle the pan to settle the batter. Bake for 20 minutes, then set aside to cool. When the pan is cool to the touch, cover it with plastic wrap and refrigerate overnight, or for a minimum of 4 to 6 hours. When ready to serve, remove the ring from the springform pan and slice into wedges. For a cleaner cut, warm the knife in hot water and dry it with a towel before cutting.

To make the candied limes, fill a medium mixing bowl with ice water.

In a medium saucepan over medium-high heat, bring 3 cups water to a boil. Add the lime slices and continue to boil for 1 minute. Remove the lime slices with a slotted spoon and submerge into the bowl of ice water to cool. When they have cooled, transfer to a paper towel to drain.

Bring 1 cup sugar and 1 cup water to a simmer in a medium saucepan over medium heat. Stir occasionally until the sugar has dissolved. Add the lime slices, being careful not to overlap them, reduce the heat to medium-low, and simmer for 1 hour.

Remove the lime slices and transfer to a wire rack to cool. Sprinkle with the remaining sugar. Shake off the excess sugar and decorate the cake by fanning the slices in a circle in the middle of the cake.

Leftover cheesecake and candied limes may be tightly covered with plastic wrap and refrigerated for up to 1 week.

MEXICAN WEDDING COOKIES
(PECAN SANDIES)

This buttery confection is commonly known as a Mexican Wedding Cookie. Happily, this recipe was handed down to me. ★ *These cookies have existed in Mexican culinary culture for centuries, in different sizes and shapes. They are traditionally served at weddings and other special occasions, and often make an appearance at Christmas celebrations.*

serves 6

2 ¼ cups all-purpose flour
¼ teaspoon salt
¾ cup coarsely ground pecans
1 cup butter, softened
½ cup powdered sugar, plus more
    to dust the baked cookies
1 teaspooon Mexican vanilla, or other
    vanilla extract

Preheat the oven to 400° F.

Combine the flour, salt, and pecans in a small mixing bowl and set aside.

Using an electric mixer on medium speed, cream the butter, sugar, and vanilla in a medium mixing bowl. Turn the mixer to low speed and slowly add the flour mixture until fully incorporated. The dough will be coarse.

Shape into 1-inch balls or small crescents. Place on a parchment paper-lined baking sheet and bake for 10 to 12 minutes. Dust the cookies with additional powdered sugar while they are still warm.

Store the cookies in an airtight container for up to 1 week.

A Cookie by Any Other Name

Perhaps you have known these delightful cookies by another name. My family always called them pecan sandies, a name that's fairly common throughout the U.S. Other names, depending on their origin, are:

Biscochitos or Biscochos, depending on the size – Mexico
Kourabiedes – Greece
Polvorones – Italy and Spain
Sand Tarts – Ukraine
Tea Cakes – Russia
Danish Wedding Cookies – Denmark

The cookies consist of simple, rich ingredients. Typically, they contain some type of nut, usually pecans. However, some versions around the globe use almonds. I recall the Danish cookie had added little bits of chocolate. But the universal factor is that each version is a light, buttery, shortbread cookie, shaped into a ball or crescent, and dusted with powdered sugar.

PEPPERED CARAMELS

Why should salted caramels get all the praise? One bite of a Peppered Caramel and you'll be hooked. These are a favorite treat to make during the holidays. They look very special when individually wrapped and placed in a pretty tin to give as a gift. ★ *Don't be afraid to add a little spice to your sweets—you can adjust the amount of spice to your taste. Dulce and picante!*

yields 64 caramels

1 cup unsalted butter, plus a little to grease the pan

2 cups dark brown sugar

1 cup light corn syrup

1 (14-ounce) can sweetened condensed milk

½ teaspoon cayenne, or more for extra heat

1 teaspoon Mexican vanilla, or other vanilla extract

Grease an 8 x 8-inch pan with butter. Also grease an 8 x 15-inch sheet of parchment with butter, and line the pan, leaving the edges of the paper overhanging a couple of inches over two sides of the pan. Butter the top side of the parchment, too.

Melt 1 cup butter in a medium saucepan over medium heat. Stir in the brown sugar, corn syrup, and sweetened condensed milk until well blended, and bring to a slow boil. Place a candy thermometer into the pan. Continue cooking over medium heat, stirring, for 20 to 30 minutes until the thermometer reads 235° F.

NOTE: Be careful not to splash the hot liquid onto the sides of the pan, it will crystalize and cause hard pieces to fall into the creamy mixture. Keep a small dish of water and a pastry brush nearby to brush down and dissolve any crystalized pieces of sugar on the sides of the pan to ensure a creamy, dreamy caramel.

Remove the pan from the heat and stir in the cayenne and the vanilla. Beat the mixture by hand until smooth and creamy. Carefully pour the hot mixture into the prepared pan and let it cool at room temperature for a minimum of 2 hours, until the caramel has set.

Lift the caramel out of the pan using the sides of the parchment paper. Use a large knife to cut the caramel into 1-inch bites. Wrap individual caramels in small pieces of parchment or wax paper, and enjoy immediately, or store in a parchment-lined, airtight container for 1 to 2 weeks.

TIP: Humid weather can often be a factor when making candy. The caramels should be firm enough to hold their shape, but should the humidity affect the outcome, place them in the refrigerator to firm up.

CREAMY PUMPKIN CANDY

My maternal grandparents were pumpkin farmers in west Texas. I've always had a weakness for anything flavored with pumpkin, and this creamy candy is one of my favorites. It has a mild pumpkin flavor and a fudge-like consistency. ★ *When my grandmother taught me how to bake a pumpkin to make pumpkin puree, I found the options were endless.* ★ *Pumpkin-flavored candy is very popular in Mexico and the Southwest, and if you haven't tasted any, try this one first.*

yields 3 dozen

Pumpkin Puree
1 small pie pumpkin
1 tablespoon vegetable oil

Candy
1 (5-ounce) can evaporated milk
2 ½ cups sugar
¾ cup pumpkin puree
1 (7-ounce) jar marshmallow cream
2 tablespoons unsalted butter, plus more
   to grease the pan
1 cup grated white chocolate, or white
   chocolate chips
1 teaspoon Mexican vanilla, or other
   vanilla extract

To make the pumpkin puree, choose a small pie pumpkin. Clean the outside with a damp paper towel. Cut the pumpkin in half from end to end with a sharp knife, and remove the seeds, membranes, and strings. (I like to clean the seeds and toast them on a baking sheet with a drizzle of olive oil and some sea salt for a healthy snack. Toast them at 375° F for 1 hour, stirring every 15 minutes.)

Brush the interior of the pumpkin halves with 1 tablespoon vegetable oil, and place the halves cut-side down on a baking sheet lined with parchment paper. Bake the pumpkin for 45 minutes in a preheated 350° F oven. Allow them to cool, then scoop the flesh out and transfer it to a blender. The outer skin will be soft and will separate easily from the flesh; discard the outer skin. Puree the pumpkin in the blender on low speed for 1 minute, or until smooth.

TIP: The pumpkin puree can be used to make pumpkin candy, pumpkin pie, Pumpkin Cornbread, (recipe, p. 26), or any recipe that calls for pumpkin puree. Refrigerate extra puree in an airtight container for up to 1 week; or freeze it in an airtight container for up to 3 months.

To make the pumpkin candy, grease a 9 x 9-inch baking pan with butter and line with a sheet of parchment paper, leaving the edges of the paper overhanging a couple of inches over the sides of the pan. Butter the top side of the parchment.

Bring the milk and sugar to a slow boil in a medium saucepan over medium heat. Stir in the pumpkin puree until smooth. Add the marshmallow cream and the butter and stir to combine. Reduce the heat to medium-low and continue cooking for 15 minutes. Remove from the heat and stir in the white chocolate and vanilla until the candy is smooth.

Pour the hot candy into the prepared pan. Allow the candy to cool at room temperature for 1 to 2 hours, until set. Once it sets, lift the candy out by the overhanging parchment paper and turn out onto a cutting board. With a large sharp knife, cut into 1 ½-inch squares.

MEXICAN CHOCOLATE PUDDING

Mexican chocolate is a little grainier than regular chocolate, and often made with the addition of other spices. It is most commonly sold in solid form in the shape of a disc. Two popular brands that are found in Latin markets and some supermarkets are Ibarra and Nestle's Abuelita; these brands can also be purchased online. ★ It's great for adding a rich, deep chocolate flavor to puddings, hot chocolate, and other desserts. This smooth, creamy pudding is further enhanced with a touch of cinnamon and cayenne.

Serves 4 to 6

¾ cup sugar

3 cups whole milk, divided

4 egg yolks

¼ cup cornstarch

6 ounces Mexican chocolate, chopped
    into small pieces

¼ teaspoon cinnamon

⅛ teaspoon cayenne, or more if you
    prefer extra heat

1 tablespoon unsalted butter, room
    temperature

1 teaspoon Mexican vanilla, or other
    vanilla extract

Combine the sugar and 2 ¾ cups milk in a medium saucepan over medium heat and bring just to a slow boil. This will take 3 to 4 minutes, so be careful not to overheat the milk. Turn the heat to low when the milk reaches a slow boil.

In a small mixing bowl, whisk together the remaining milk, egg yolks, and cornstarch until smooth. Temper the egg yolk mixture by whisking in a small amount of the warm milk to bring up the temperature of the eggs. Gradually add the egg mixture to the milk in the saucepan, whisking until combined. Stir in the chocolate pieces until they are melted. Whisk in the cinnamon and cayenne, then raise the heat to medium and bring the mixture to a slow boil again. Cook for 3 minutes, stirring constantly, until the mixture thickens. When the pudding coats the back of the spoon and stays in place when you run your finger down it, remove the pan from the heat and immediately stir in the butter and vanilla until smooth. It will continue to thicken as it cools.

Serve at room temperature, or chilled for a firmer consistency.

Leftover pudding may be refrigerated in an airtight container for up to 1 week, or make ahead and refrigerate until you are ready to serve.

CINNAMON ICE CREAM

Homemade ice cream is quick and easy to make with a little countertop ice cream or yogurt maker. I like to use one that has a cylinder you can keep chilled in the freezer, so it's cold when I'm ready to whip up a batch. ★ *In less than half an hour, you can be scooping Cinnamon Ice Cream over a delicious bowl of Buttery Rum Bananas, Mangos, and Pineapple (recipe, p. 140). It's the perfect treat to cool your palate after a spicy meal. Or serve it over your favorite cobbler after a plate of bold Texas barbecue.*

serves 8

3 cups half & half
1 ½ cups whole milk
¾ cup sugar
¼ cup light brown sugar
¼ cup honey
1 tablespoon Mexican vanilla, or
   other vanilla extract
2 teaspoons cinnamon

In a large mixing bowl, whisk together all ingredients by hand or with an electric mixer, until the sugar is dissolved.

Pour the mixture into the ice cream freezer container. Insert the paddle and cover with the lid. Set the machine to freeze for 20 to 25 minutes for soft-serve ice cream. If a firmer consistency is desired, transfer to an airtight container, and freeze for a minimum of 2 hours.

Leftover ice cream can be stored in an airtight container in the freezer for up to 3 weeks.

GRANDPA JOE'S SOPAPILLAS

Sopapillas are a quick bread that originated in New Mexico more than 200 years ago, although there are other versions of the same type of bread from other countries. The word sopapilla loosely translates to "holding soup". As they fry, they puff up into soft pillows. My husband's father, who was from New Mexico, would make them when he and his siblings were young. They would tear off a corner and squeeze honey into the soft pillows of dough. ★ *Sopapillas are most commonly served as a dessert throughout the Southwest. They may be sprinkled with cinnamon and sugar, or dusted with powder sugar, and they pair well with a bowl of fresh berries or fresh, diced peaches.*

yields 16

2 cups all-purpose flour, plus more
   for dusting

1 teaspoon salt

1 teaspoon baking powder

2 tablespoons vegetable oil, plus more
   for frying

¼ cup milk, room temperature

Honey, to pass around the table

In a medium mixing bowl, whisk together the flour, salt, and baking powder. Work 2 tablespoons oil into the flour mixture with your hands. Add ½ cup lukewarm water and the milk, stirring until just combined, and the dough comes together. Turn the dough out onto a lightly floured surface and knead by hand for 5 minutes. Cover with a damp cloth and let the dough rest for 5 minutes.

After 5 minutes, divide the dough into 4 balls, again cover with a damp cloth, and let the dough balls rest for another 5 minutes.

Heat 1 ½-inches of oil in a deep skillet over medium heat.

Using a floured rolling pin, roll the dough balls out into ¼-inch thick circles. Cut each circle into quarters.

Using a deep fry thermometer, check the heat of the oil. When it reaches 400° F, fry the sopapillas, 3 or 4 at time. When they float to the top of the oil, cook for 2 minutes, checking to see that the bottoms are turning brown. Spoon the hot oil over the top of the dough while the bottom side is browning. Within 2 minutes, the bottoms should be golden brown. Gently flip them over and continue cooking for 2 minutes, until the other side is browned. Use a slotted spoon or spider to remove the sopapillas, and transfer them to a paper towel-lined baking sheet to drain. Repeat the process for the remaining sopapillas.

Serve warm with honey. Sopapillas may be made 1 hour prior to serving, and kept warm in a 200° F oven.

Leftover sopapillas may be refrigerated in a zip-top bag for up to 1 week, and reheated in a 350° oven for 10 to 15 minutes.

BUNUELOS

Bunuelos are a bit of a cross between flour tortillas and sopapillas. They are popular to eat on New Year's Eve for good luck in the year ahead, but they are really enjoyed all year long. They are typically rolled out into circles but will taste just as good in other shapes. ★ *Since Bunuelos are fried, I like to save this decadent treat for special occasions—great to serve for a party!*

yields 20

3 cups all-purpose flour
1 teaspoon baking powder
1 teaspoon salt
2 teaspoons cinnamon, divided
¾ cup milk
¼ cup unsalted butter
1 teaspoon Mexican vanilla, or other vanilla extract
2 eggs, beaten
Vegetable oil for frying
⅓ cup sugar

Mix the flour, baking powder, salt, and 1 teaspoon cinnamon in a large bowl and set aside.

Place the milk, butter and vanilla in a medium saucepan over medium heat and bring to a slow boil for 3 to 4 minutes. Remove from the heat.

Temper the beaten eggs with 2 or 3 tablespoons hot milk mixture before adding the eggs to the rest of the hot milk; this will keep the eggs from cooking in the hot liquid. Whisk until well blended. Slowly add the milk and egg mixture to the dry ingredients.

Mix until the dough comes together in a ball. Turn the dough onto a floured surface and knead for 2 to 3 minutes. Divide the dough into 20 balls.

Add approximately 1 inch of vegetable oil to a medium skillet over medium heat. Roll the dough balls out into 6- or 7-inch diameter circles.

Drop a small pinch of dough into the oil to test if it's hot enough to fry. When the dough sizzles, fry the bunuelos one at a time, for 1 to 2 minutes on one side, then flip and fry for 1 minute on the other side, or until they begin to bubble in places and turn brown. With a slotted spoon, remove the bunuelos from the skillet and stand them upright in a paper towel-lined bowl to drain.

Sprinkle with a mixture of 1 teaspoon cinnamon and the sugar while the bunuelos are still hot. Serve them at room temperature.

Bunuelos may be stored in an airtight container at room temperature for 3 to 4 days.

DULCE DE LECHE, TWO WAYS

Dulce de Leche is sweetened milk slowly reduced to a thick caramel-like sauce. It is used in many desserts across the Southwest and other parts of the world. Serve it as a dip for fresh fruit, or drizzle it over Cinnamon Ice Cream (recipe, p. 151). ★ Dulce de Leche can be made in a variety of ways. These are the the two methods I like best. First is the milk and sugar cooked slowly on the stovetop; the second method conveniently starts with cans of sweetened condensed milk in the slow-cooker. This lets the magic happen while I focus on other things in the kitchen. If you use the slow-cooker method, it's best to use more than 1 can. The contents of 2 cans make enough Dulce de Leche to fill 3 (½-pint) jars. I keep one for myself and give the others as gifts.

Stovetop Method
yields ¾ cup

2 cups whole milk
¾ cup sugar
1 teaspoon Mexican vanilla, or other
    vanilla extract
¼ teaspoon baking soda

Slow-cooker Method
yields 1 ½ pints

2 (14-ounce) cans sweetened condensed
    milk
3 (½-pint) canning jars with tightly
    sealed lids

For the stovetop method: Whisk together the milk, sugar, and vanilla in a medium saucepan over medium heat. Bring to a simmer, stirring, just until the sugar dissolves. Add the baking soda and stir to combine. Reduce the heat to medium-low and cook for 2 hours, stirring occasionally (avoid scraping down the sides of the pan where the mixture is thicker), until the liquid turns a dark golden brown color and thickens. The milk should reduce to ¾ cup.

Allow to cool before serving. Dulce de Leche may be served chilled, or at room temperature, and may be refrigerated in an airtight container for up to 1 month.

For the slow-cooker method: Pour the contents of the 2 cans condensed milk into 3 (½-pint) jars. Tightly seal the lids on the jars and place the jars into a slow-cooker, with enough water to cover the jars. Cook on high for 8 or 9 hours. Check after 8 hours to see that the color is a dark golden brown. If the color of the milk remains light, continue cooking on high for 1 to 2 hours.

Remove the jars from the slow-cooker with tongs and dry them with a kitchen towel. Allow the jars to cool, then refrigerate them.

Serve the Dulce de Leche chilled, or at room temperature. The jars may be refrigerated after opening, and kept for up to 1 month.

MANZANAS EN VINO
(APPLES IN WINE)

An apple a day is always a good thing. Baked apples with cinnamon, butter, and pecans is an intoxicating combination all on its own, but basting the apples with wine makes them even better. ★ *Manzanas en Vino can also be drizzled with Dulce de Leche (recipe, p. 154), or topped off with Cinnamon Ice Cream (recipe, p. 151) for a really special dessert.*

serves 4

4 good baking apples, washed and cored
4 teaspoons unsalted butter
4 cinnamon sticks
4 tablespoons brown sugar
¼ cup pecans, chopped
2 teaspoons raisins, optional
I cup white wine

Preheat the oven to 350° F.

Stand the apples upright in a shallow baking dish. If any of the apples are a little lopsided, cut the bottom so that they will stand upright.

Place I teaspoon butter into the opening of each apple, and insert I cinnamon stick into each. Sprinkle I tablespoon brown sugar around the cinnamon sticks. Add a few pieces of pecans and some raisins to each apple, if desired. Pour the wine into the bottom of the baking dish.

Bake for 45 minutes, basting the apples with the wine in the dish after 25 minutes.

Remove the cinnamon sticks, place each apple in a small serving bowl, and spoon the juice from the bottom of the baking dish around each apple. Top with Dulce de Leche or Cinnamon Ice Cream, as desired.

Leftover apples may be refrigerated in an airtight container for up to I week. To reheat, wrap them in foil and bake in a 350° F oven for 15 minutes, or until heated through.

KICKSTART BREAKFASTS

Start your morning with a spicy bite of goodness

MIGAS

Migas gets its name from the Spanish and Portuguese word for "crumbs." It's a great way to use up bits and pieces of leftover tortillas. This egg dish is served for breakfast all over the Southwest, and is even popular served as tapas. ★ It can be served meatless, or topped with crispy pieces of bacon and grated cheese. Add fresh cilantro leaves and Charred Salsa (recipe, p. 41), as desired.

serves 4

4 corn tortillas, cut into 1-inch squares
2 tablespoons vegetable oil
8 eggs
3 tablespoons milk
¼ teaspoon salt
¼ teaspoon black pepper
1 tablespoon butter
1 fresh jalapeño, stemmed, seeded, and
    finely diced

Optional Toppings
Grated cheese
Crispy bacon
Cilantro leaves
Charred Salsa (recipe, p. 41)

Stack the tortillas and cut them into 1-inch squares. Heat the oil in a medium skillet over medium heat and add the tortilla pieces, stirring to coat. Cook 1 to 2 minutes, until they just begin to brown. Transfer the tortillas to a paper towel-lined plate to drain.

Whisk together the eggs, milk, salt, and pepper in a small bowl and set aside.

Melt the butter in a large skillet over medium heat and add the jalapeño. Whisk in the egg mixture and cook for 1 minute. Stir in the tortilla pieces and cook another 1 to 2 minutes, or until the eggs are done to your preference.

Plate the migas with any desired toppings and serve warm.

Leftovers may be refrigerated in an airtight container for 1 to 2 days. Reheat leftovers in a microwave-safe dish in 20 second intervals in a microwave until heated through.

ZUCCHINI MUFFINS
WITH TOASTED PEPITAS (PUMPKIN SEEDS)

One spring I bought what I thought was a mix of zucchini and yellow squash plants for my garden. But when they started producing, they were all yellow squash. I told my neighbor about this disappointment. Then a strange thing happened: I found two huge zucchini in my garden! It turns out my neighbor sneakily placed them there next to the yellow squash to fool me. I enjoyed both the laugh and the zucchini bread I made with them. I even took the neighbor a loaf; he said he might have to sneak zucchini into my garden more often. ★ If you grow zucchini and occasionally let them get too big before you harvest them, a good remedy is to remove the large, hardened seeds and the tough peel. Then grate the remainder to use in recipes like this one for zucchini muffins. ★ These taste great with glass of orange juice or a cup of Creamy Atole (recipe, p. 181).

serves 6

3 cups all-purpose flour
1 tablespoon cinnamon
1 teaspoon baking soda
½ teaspoon salt
¼ teaspoon baking powder
¾ cup pepitas (pumpkin seeds)
2 cups sugar
1 cup vegetable oil
3 eggs, beaten
1 tablespoon vanilla extract
3 cups grated zucchini (see TIP
    at right)

Crumble Topping
⅓ cup toasted pepitas
4 tablespoons sugar
½ cup all-purpose flour
4 tablespoons cold butter, cut
    into small cubes

Spray 18 muffin tin cups with non-stick spray, or line them with cupcake liners.

Sift together the flour, cinnamon, baking soda, salt, and baking powder, and set aside.

Preheat the oven to 350° F.

Toast the pepitas for both the batter and the topping in a dry skillet over medium heat for 5 minutes or until lightly browned, stirring occasionally. Set aside to cool, then divide into the designated portions for the muffin batter and the topping.

In the bowl of an electric mixer, add the sugar, oil, and eggs and blend on medium speed until smooth. Add the vanilla and mix well. Slowly add the flour mixture to the batter just until well combined. With the mixer on low, slowly add the grated zucchini and ¾ cup toasted pepitas. Evenly distribute the batter with a standard-size ice cream scoop into the muffin tins.

To make the crumble topping, roughly chop the remaining ⅓ cup toasted pepitas, and transfer to a small mixing bowl. Stir in the sugar and flour. Use a pastry cutter, or 2 butter knives, and cut the cold butter pieces into the topping. Sprinkle by spoonful over each muffin. Bake for 22 to 25 minutes, or until a tooth pick comes out clean when inserted in the center of a muffin.

NOTE: If using a smaller zucchini which has a tender peel and seeds, you may grate the entire zucchini. For a larger zucchini, peel and seed it before grating. Also, grating zucchini may produce a little liquid. You will especially notice this if you are using zucchini that has been frozen and thawed. If the moisture seems excessive, press some of the liquid out between paper towels.

TIP: When you can't bake right away, my mom has always suggested to go ahead and grate the zucchini and place it in a freezer bag. It will keep in the freezer for up to six months. I use it for a nice treat during the wintertime when my garden is long gone.

BREAKFAST TACOS

Breakfast tacos are the real deal when it comes to a quick protein-filled breakfast. They are phenomenally popular, sold from taco trucks all over the Southwest, and throughout many regions of the country. With this easy recipe, you won't have to wave down the taco truck tomorrow morning. ★ *Serve with a steaming cup of Café con Chocolate (recipe, p. 176).*

serves 4 to 6

2 tablespoons olive oil

2 new potatoes, cleaned and diced

½ teaspoon dried Mexican oregano, or other oregano

½ teaspoon crushed red pepper flakes

¼ teaspoon salt

¼ teaspoon black pepper

2 ounces Serrano ham slices, diced

4 eggs

1 teaspoon butter

6 Handmade Corn Tortillas (recipe p. 28), or Handmade Flour Tortillas (recipe, p. 30)

Charred Salsa (recipe, p. 41)

Heat the olive oil in a large skillet over medium heat and add the potatoes. Season them with the oregano, red pepper flakes, salt, and pepper. Add the Serrano ham and cook for 15 minutes, stirring occasionally, until the ham is crisp and the potatoes are tender.

While the ham and potatoes are cooking, whisk the eggs in a small mixing bowl. Push the potato mixture to one side of the skillet and add the butter to the empty side. When the butter melts, pour in the eggs and scramble them for 2 to 3 minutes on their side of the skillet, until they are almost done. Stir the eggs and potatoes together and set the skillet aside.

Heat the tortillas in a hot, dry skillet over medium heat for 20 to 30 seconds on each side. Fill each tortilla with the egg and potato mixture, top with salsa as needed, and serve warm.

Leftovers may be refrigerated in an airtight container for 1 to 2 days. Reheat leftovers in a damp paper towel in the microwave in 20 second intervals until heated through.

DELMONICO STEAKS
WITH PAPAS AND GREEN CHILE GRAVY

Delmonico steak is the name for a cut of beef from the rib or short-loin. There are many versions of what a Delmonico steak is and should be, but it was first served around 1850 in a New York steak house called Delmonico's, and quickly became famous. ★ *This steak is full of flavor and very tender and can be cooked quickly, so it is an excellent choice for a special breakfast, especially paired with papas and green chile.*

serves 6

¼ cup vegetable oil

4 Russet potatoes, cleaned, peeled, and diced

4 (7-ounce) Delmonico steaks

I teaspoon salt, divided

I teaspoon black pepper, divided

I tablespoon unsalted butter

¾ cup Western Green Chile (recipe, p. 39)

½ cup beef broth

Heat the oil in a cast-iron skillet over medium heat. Test the heat of the oil by dropping 1 piece of potato into the skillet; when it sizzles, add the rest. Season the potatoes with ½ teaspoon salt and ½ teaspoon black pepper. Cook for 15 minutes, stirring occasionally, until the potatoes are golden brown and tender. Drain the potatoes on a paper towel-lined baking sheet, and place in a 200° F oven to keep them warm.

Increase the heat under the skillet to medium-high. Season the steaks with the remaining salt and black pepper, and sear them in the skillet for 1 minute on each side. (If the steaks crowd the skillet, cook them in 2 batches, so as not to "steam" the steaks; if the skillet is overcrowded, the steaks will not sear or brown well.)

Reduce the heat to medium and continue cooking for approximately 4 minutes per side, depending on how done you like your steaks. Transfer the cooked steaks to the baking sheet with the potatoes to keep them warm in the oven.

In the same skillet, melt the butter and scrape up any brown bits from the bottom of the skillet. Add the Western Green Chile and beef broth, and stir to combine. Cook for 2 to 3 minutes, or until heated through.

Divide the potatoes between 4 dinner plates. Place a steak atop the potatoes and top with the green chile gravy.

Leftover steak may be stored in an airtight container in the refrigerator for up to 1 week. Reheat leftovers in a skillet over medium heat for 4 to 5 minutes, or until heated through.

TORTILLA DE CHORIZO

A Spanish tortilla is similar to an omelet and typically contains eggs and potatoes. It can also be compared to a potato pancake or an Italian frittata. It makes a great breakfast for a leisurely weekend morning, and is fantastic for brunch, served either warm or at room temperature. The Spanish chorizo in this recipe is a cured sausage. ★ *Serve with a frosty glass of Agua de la Fruta (recipe, p. 182).*

serves 4

3 ounces Spanish chorizo, sliced into
¼-inch rounds

3 small new potatoes, sliced into ¼-inch
rounds

2 tablespoons diced Spanish onion, or
other onion

4 eggs, beaten

½ cup half & half

¼ teaspoon salt

¼ teaspoon black pepper

½ cup grated Monterey jack, or pepper
jack cheese

Preheat the oven to 425° F.

Heat a 10- to 12-inch ovenproof skillet (cast-iron works well) over medium heat and add the chorizo. When a small amount of fat has rendered, add the potato slices and the onion. Cook for 10 minutes, stirring occasionally, or until the potatoes are tender.

In a small mixing bowl, whisk together the eggs, half & half, salt, and pepper. When the potatoes are almost done, pour the egg mixture into the skillet over the chorizo and potatoes, and continue cooking for 1 minute.

Sprinkle the grated cheese evenly over the top of the egg mixture and transfer the skillet to the preheated oven. Bake for 4 to 5 minutes until the eggs puff up and set.

Cut into quarters and serve warm or at room temperature.

Leftovers may be refrigerated in an airtight container for 1 to 2 days. Reheat leftovers on a microwave-safe plate in 20 second intervals until heated through.

GREEN CHILE BREAKFAST BOWL

On the weekend we're looking for something high in protein to start our day with a real kick, right? Green Chile Breakfast Bowls will give you the energy you need for all your weekend activities. ★ *Serve with an ice cold glass of Naranja Horchata (recipe, p. 174).*

serves 4

½ pound Mexican Breakfast Chorizo
    (recipe, p. 167), crumbled
8 eggs
2 tablespoons milk
¼ teaspoon salt
¼ teaspoon black pepper
1 tablespoon unsalted butter
1 cup Western Green Chile, (recipe p. 39)
½ cup grated cheddar cheese

In a medium skillet, cook the breakfast chorizo over medium heat for 10 minutes, or until browned and cooked through. Drain on a paper towel-lined plate, and set the chorizo aside.

In a small mixing bowl, whisk together the eggs, milk, salt, and pepper.

Melt the butter in a separate skillet over medium heat. Add the eggs and scramble them for 2 to 3 minutes, until they are done to your preference.

Heat the Western Green Chile in a small saucepan over medium heat for 4 to 5 minutes, until heated through.

Layer the eggs and chorizo in 4 serving bowls and top with Western Green Chile, and the grated cheese. Serve warm.

Leftovers may be refrigerated in an airtight container for 1 to 2 days. Reheat leftovers in a microwave-safe bowl in 30 second intervals until heated though.

MEXICAN BREAKFAST CHORIZO

Spanish-style chorizo is a cured sausage. Mexican-style chorizo is a soft sausage, typically squeezed from the casing and crumbled into a skillet and browned. This type is very simple to make at home without casings. I like to make an extra batch to freeze; just shape the chorizo into patties and flash freeze on a baking sheet, then place them in a zip-top freezer bag. You can handily pull out the amount you need for breakfast. ★ If you do not have a meat grinder, ask your butcher to prepare a package of ground pork butt. With this method you will know exactly what goes into it. You can control the amount of spice, and you can reduce the amount of fat, if you ask the butcher to trim the pork butt. But be sure to leave a little fat for flavor. Serve patties as a breakfast protein or crumbled and browned in recipes like Green Chile Breakfast Bowls (recipe, p. 166).

yields I pound

I pound freshly ground pork butt
2 tablespoons apple cider vinegar
I to 2 tablespoons chili powder, to taste
I tablespoon smoked paprika
I teaspoon dried Mexican oregano, or
    other oregano
½ teaspoon crushed red pepper flakes
¼ teaspoon salt
¼ teaspoon cumin
¼ teaspoon garlic powder

In a medium mixing bowl, combine the ground pork, apple cider vinegar, and spices by hand or with an electric mixer fitted with a paddle attachment.

Shape the mixture into patties, or crumble for browning to add to scrambled eggs, breakfast burritos, or potatoes.

Cook the patties, or crumbled chorizo, in a large skillet over medium heat for 10 minutes, or until browned and cooked through.

Chorizo sealed in a zip-top freezer bag may be frozen for up to 3 months. Refrigerate cooked sausage in an airtight container for up to 2 days. Reheat leftovers in a skillet over medium heat for 4 to 5 minutes, or until heated through.

THIRST QUENCHERS

*Cool off (or warm up) with drinks infused
with Southwest flavors*

PRICKLY PEAR MARGARITA

Prickly pears are a beautiful fruit or "berry" that grows on several varieties of cacti in Texas and the Southwest. These yellow, orange, or purple berries are in season from late summer to early winter. Gathering and processing them is an ambitious undertaking, given the stinging cactus needles that must be avoided, but the tasty juice they render has a mild melon scent and flavor and goes well with Southwestern cuisine. ★ Since they can be difficult to find in some regions of the country, I have used prickly pear syrup, available at most well-stocked liquor stores, as a great alternative.

yields 2 drinks

2 ounces tequila blanco

2 ounces prickly pear juice, or syrup

½ ounce triple sec, plus 1 tablespoon to coat the rim of the glass

3 tablespoons fresh lime juice

2 teaspoons coarse salt

2 teaspoons turbinado sugar

Pour the tequila, prickly pear juice or syrup, triple sec, and lime juice into a drink shaker with ½ cup ice cubes. Shake to chill.

Mix the salt and turbinado sugar together on a saucer. Place a tablespoon of triple sec in another saucer. Dip the rims of 2 glasses into the triple sec and then into the salt-sugar mixture.

Strain the margarita mixture into the glasses and serve immediately.

GRAPEFRUIT-AGAVE PALOMA

A Paloma is an elegant drink that commonly consists of tequila and grapefruit soda. When a Paloma is made with grapefruit juice, it is often sweetened with sugar. This one is made with both freshly squeezed grapefruit juice and agave nectar and is irresistible. ★ *Enjoy this cocktail by itself, or with a plate of Green Chile Chicken Enchiladas (recipe, p. 110).*

yields 1 drink

1 ounce tequila
¼ cup fresh grapefruit juice
1 teaspoon agave nectar, found in most
   supermarkets near the honey section
½ teaspoon fresh lime juice
½ cup club soda
1 slice lime, for garnish

In a small pitcher, combine the tequila, grapefruit juice, agave nectar, and lime juice. Add the soda and stir to combine. Pour over ice and serve immediately. Garnish with a slice of lime.

NARANJA HORCHATA

Horchata is a milky drink often made from rice, and served chilled, over ice. It often contains cinnamon and vanilla. This one goes a step further with the addition of fresh orange zest. Hochata is available in Mexican markets around the Southwest, chilled in large glass containers and ladled into paper cups. ★ *It's refreshing as a mid-afternoon snack, or served with Breakfast Tacos (recipe, p. 162).*

yields about 1 quart

2 cups white long grain rice, uncooked

1 stick canela (a thin, flaky Mexican cinnamon)

4 cups whole milk

1 tablespoon Mexican vanilla, or other vanilla extract

2 (14-ounce) cans sweetened condensed milk

Zest of 2 oranges

Place the rice, 3 cups hot water, and the cinnamon stick into a large pitcher. Cover with a lid or plastic wrap and leave on the countertop overnight.

The next morning, pour the rice and water mixture into a blender and blend on high for 1 to 2 minutes until the rice is pulverized. Strain the liquid into a large, wide-mouth jar.

Add the milk, vanilla, sweetened condensed milk, and orange zest to the jar and stir to combine.

Ladle into cups and serve over ice, or refrigerate until you are ready to serve.

Horchata may be refrigerated, covered, for 2 to 3 days.

CAFÉ CON CHOCOLATE

Coffee and chocolate are combined in Café con Chocolate to create a concoction that will warm you from head to toe. The warmth of the cinnamon and sweetness of the chocolate and brown sugar make this a favorite in the Southwest. ★ This recipe gives you two ways to make this delicious drink; on the stovetop or with a French press.

serves 4 to 6

¼ cup light brown sugar
1 stick canela (a thin, flaky Mexican
   cinnamon)
½ cup ground coffee beans
½ teaspoon Mexican vanilla, or
   other vanilla extract
2 ounces Mexican chocolate, or
   semi-sweet chocolate, grated
Whipped cream and cinnamon or nutmeg,
   to garnish

For the stovetop version: Bring 6 cups water, the sugar and cinnamon stick to a boil in a small saucepan over medium heat. Remove the pan from the heat and add the ground coffee beans. Stir in the vanilla and chocolate. Cover with the lid and let the mixture steep for 5 minutes. Discard the cinnamon stick. Strain through a mesh sieve into mugs.

For the French press version: Bring 6 cups water, the sugar, and cinnamon stick to a boil in a saucepan over medium heat. Remove the pan from the heat and stir in the vanilla and chocolate. Place the ground coffee beans in the bottom of a 6-cup French press, or make individual servings if you have a smaller press. Fill the press container with the hot liquid and let it steep for 5 minutes. Discard the cinnamon stick. Push the handle on the press down.

Serve hot topped with whipped cream and a dash of cinnamon or nutmeg.

Leftovers can be placed in an airtight container and refrigerated for up to 1 week. Reheat leftover Café Con Chocolate in a small saucepan over medium heat for 5 minutes or until heated through.

PEACHY SANGRIA

There is hardly anything more refreshing under the hot Texas sun than a chilled glass of fruit-filled sangria. This one is a sangria blanca, or sangria made with white wine. It's loaded with fresh fruit and is the ultimate beverage to serve at a backyard barbecue. ★ *Pair it with Gulf Coast Street Tacos (recipe, p. 126), or Blackened Chicken Tacos (recipe, p. 116).*

serves 8 to 10

2 fresh peaches
2 small oranges
2 limes
¼ honey dew melon, peeled, seeded, and cut into bite-size pieces
½ cup fresh red raspberries
¼ cup fresh mint leaves
1 tablespoon sugar
2 (750 ml) bottles crisp white wine, such as a Riesling, or Pinot Grigio
3 tablespoons honey

Rinse all the fruit under cool water and pat dry with a paper towel.

Cut the peaches into wedges and place half the wedges into a 2-quart pitcher.

Cut 1 orange and 1 lime into thin slices and add to pitcher.

Juice the remaining orange and lime and add the juice to the pitcher. Add the honey dew melon and raspberries.

In a small bowl, mix the mint leaves with sugar and slightly crush the mint with the back of a spoon, then add to the pitcher.

Add the wine and honey to the pitcher and stir to combine.

Chill for at least 1 hour to allow the flavors to combine. When you are ready to serve, use the remaining peach wedges to garnish the glasses. Served chilled.

Leftovers may be refrigerated for up to 2 days.

SPICY MICHELADA

This Michelada is a Mexican cerveza, spiced up and served ice-cold with a salted rim. ★ *It's a great party drink to serve with snacks like Fresh Corn Tortilla Chips (recipe, p. 20) and Loaded Guacamole (recipe, p. 21). And it goes well with Mesquite Smoked Brisket (recipe, p. 96).*

yields 2 drinks

2 (12-ounce) Mexican beers

1 (5 ½-ounce) can vegetable juice, such as V-8

3 teaspoons hot sauce, your choice brand

3 teaspoons fresh lime juice, plus extra to coat the rims of the glasses

1 ½ teaspoons Worcestershire sauce

¼ teaspoon black pepper

⅛ teaspoon cayenne

1 teaspoon lime zest

1 teaspoon coarse salt

2 pickled jalapeño slices, for garnish

In a small pitcher or shaker, mix together the beer, vegetable juice, hot sauce, lime juice, and Worcestershire sauce. Add the black pepper and cayenne and mix well.

In a small saucer, combine the lime zest and salt. Moisten the rims of 2 beer glasses with lime juice, then dip the rims in the lime zest-salt mixture. Serve with or without ice. Fill each glass with the spicy cerveza, garnish with a slice of jalapeño, and serve immediately.

MANGO MOJITO

A mojito is a beautiful, fragrant cocktail that is often mixed with other flavors. ★ *The addition of mango makes this the ultimate tropical drink to serve before dinner with Fresh Corn Tortilla Chips (recipe, p. 20) and Grilled Avocado Salsa (recipe, p. 18).*

yields 1 drink

3 teaspoons sugar

8 fresh mint leaves

2 tablespoons fresh lime juice

¼ cup cubed mango (see "Cubing a Mango," p. 34)

2 ounces light rum, your choice brand

2 ounces club soda

½ cup crushed ice

1 sprig fresh mint, for garnish

Place the sugar and mint leaves into a small bowl or pitcher. Muddle the mixture with a muddler or a wooden spoon, releasing the oils from the mint and crushing the sugar and mint together.

Add lime juice and mango and continue muddling, crushing the mango against the sides of the pitcher. The mixture should have a bit of texture.

Add the rum and soda and stir to mix. Pour over crushed ice and serve immediately. Garnish with a fresh sprig of mint.

CREAMY ATOLE

Atole is of Mexican origin. It is a creamy drink, served warm. It's made with corn masa and usually served with dishes like Chicken Verde Tamales (recipe, p. 124). It also makes a great accompaniment to Green Chile Breakfast Bowl (recipe, p. 166). ★ *The corn masa brings a whole new element to how we think of making warm drinks.*

yields 4 drinks

¼ cup masa harina, found in most supermarkets near the all-purpose flour

1 teaspoon cinnamon

2 tablespoons piloncillo sugar, or light brown sugar

1 teaspoon Mexican vanilla, or other vanilla extract

Whisk the masa harina together with 2 ½ cups water in a medium saucepan. Add the cinnamon and sugar, stirring to combine, and bring to a slow boil over medium heat. Reduce the heat to medium-low and simmer for 5 minutes.

Remove the pan from the heat and whisk in the vanilla extract. Serve immediately.

AGUA DE LA FRUTA
WITH PINEAPPLE

Cold fruit drinks, called agua frescas or agua de la frutas, are made with fresh fruit, water and crushed ice. They can also contain fresh herbs and spices. ★ *This version is popular with young and old alike, and a healthy treat with the refreshingly tart taste of fresh pineapple.*

serves 4

1 pineapple, peeled, cored, and cut into
   (4 cups) 1-inch chunks
1 cup sugar
3 tablespoons fresh lime juice

Place the pineapple, sugar, 6 cups water, and lime juice in a blender, and blend on medium speed for 30 to 60 seconds. Pour over crushed ice and serve immediately.

Re-stir if the drink sits a while before serving.

HIBISCUS CITRUS-INFUSED ICED TEA

Tea made from hibiscus flowers already contains notes of citrus. When infused with orange, lemon, and lime, this tea goes from good to great. ★ *I like to serve it with my favorite Southwestern dishes, such as Carne Asada (recipe, p. 100).*

serves 6

4 hibiscus (red zinger) tea bags
½ cup agave nectar, found in most
   supermarkets near the honey section
1 orange, sliced into ½-inch rounds
1 lemon, sliced into ½-inch rounds
1 lime, sliced into ½-inch rounds

In a tea kettle or medium saucepan, bring 4 cups of water to a boil over medium-high heat.

Place the tea bags into a 2-quart pitcher and cover with boiling water. Let them steep for 10 minutes, then remove and discard the tea bags.

Add the agave nectar and stir to combine. Add the citrus slices and let the tea rest for 1 hour to infuse the flavors.

When you are ready to serve, add enough water to fill the pitcher, and serve over ice.

The leftover tea may be refrigerated for 3 to 4 days.

COZY MEXICAN COCOA

When my daughter was really young, she wrote out a little recipe for making hot chocolate that she called "cozy cocoa." I love that name. It was made with a sprinkle of cinnamon and a hint of vanilla. The warm, rich flavor of Mexican chocolate partners well with these ingredients for an unforgettable cup of Mexican hot chocolate that I call Cozy Mexican Cocoa. ★ *Serve it with Bunuelos (recipe, p. 153).*

yields 2 cups

2 cups whole milk
1 tablespoon grated piloncillo sugar, or
   brown sugar
4 ½ ounces Mexican chocolate, chopped
½ teaspoon Mexican vanilla, or other
   vanilla extract
⅛ teaspoon cinnamon
1 pinch cayenne, optional

Combine the milk and sugar in a small saucepan over medium heat and warm for 2 to 3 minutes, taking care not to let the milk boil. Remove the pan from the heat and stir in the chocolate, vanilla, cinnamon, and cayenne, if you prefer a little heat.

Return the pan to the stovetop over medium heat, and cook for 1 to 2 minutes, stirring, until the chocolate is completely melted.

Pour into cups and serve warm.

INDEX

ACKNOWLEDGMENTS

Michael, a.k.a. stud muffin husband, you have cheered me on, soothed my tears, rubbed my tired shoulders and taste tested endless amounts of Southwestern Cuisine, and all with that sweet, mischievous smile on your face. Thank you for the many tortilla presses you have constructed and the numerous times you have demonstrated your fabulous grilling skills to prepare many of these dishes. I could not accomplish this without you.

Tuesday, my beautiful daughter, I could never thank you enough for your expertise, attention to detail, and inspiration. You tirelessly helped prepare the food we tested and photographed for this book and I am forever in your debt. You are a genius in the kitchen! I love you so much, my sweet girl.

Nick, my handsome son, your loving support, witty humor, and constant encouragement has kept me on point. I love that you have become such a wonderful cook, in your own right. Thank you for making me a proud mama. Love and hugs.

Christina and Michelle, I am so grateful to have you girls in my life. Thank you to you and to your beautiful families for your love and support. I appreciate the encouragement and I am so inspired by the two of you. I cherish our relationships and every discussion about making pies, cakes, doughnuts, cookies and tortillas. Lots of love.

Janice Shay, my agent, editor, designer, and book packager extraordinaire—you have negotiated, coached, and guided my way through this beautiful project. Thank you for your faith in me. You may be a Georgia girl now, but I hope you will always be a Texan at heart.

Deborah Whitlaw Llewellyn, thank you for making the colors of the Southwest come to life in this book. The gorgeous photos tell as much of a story as the recipes do. You have precisely captured the experience I want to share with everyone who reads The Whole Enchilada.

A Texas-size thank you goes to Margot Hardin at Stuffology in Crosbyton, Texas, and to Kim Sparks at Jux-Ta-Posh in Lubbock for the use of all the beautiful photo props you provided. I am so grateful!

Bonnie LaRue, my very first lessons in cooking came from you. I am so fortunate I was raised by a mother who cooked 3 solid meals, almost every day. Our family time around the table has always been the best of times. Hanging out in the kitchen, making peanut butter balls, and discussing recipes is one of my favorite things in life. Mike, Rhonda, Mackenzie, and Autumn I don't know what I would possibly do if I didn't have you to lean on, and to taste all my experiments. Missy, I'm so lucky you and Dub came into my life; I will always treasure the experience we gained from watching Dub in the kitchen. Danny, Rudy, Susan and fam, your stories of Mexican cuisine, pralines, chile, and tacos will always peak my interest – gracias!

At left: my daughter, Tuesday.

My love and appreciation also go to my hardworking grandparents, my lovely aunts and uncles, and all my many cousins. There are so many fantastic cooks in my family. How wonderful life is, and has been, to experience it with you. The importance of all the family gatherings we once took for granted is now realized. To share these moments with you has made me a very blessed and happy girl. There is no better place to be than around the family table.

Daddy, your love of Blanco Canyon is where it all started. I love you and I miss you.

Top row: Grandpa and Grandma Lightner; Above: Grandma Lowe, PaPaw Dub, my mom, Bonnie LaRue, and my dad, Johnny.

My son, Nick.

My husband, Michael.